COOK'S COLLECTION

GLUTEN FREE

*Fuss-free and tasty recipe ideas
for the modern cook*

CONTENTS

INTRODUCTION

Going gluten free, whatever the reason, doesn't need to be daunting. There are endless options for gluten-free food, including a wide-range of gluten-free alternatives and much of the food you already eat. Any worries you might have about missing out on your favourite foods can be thrown out – the range of recipes here is as varied as it is delicious.

Coeliac disease, the most common reason to follow a gluten-free diet, is a complete intolerance to gluten, a protein found in wheat, rye, barley and spelt. Even a tiny amount of gluten will have a bad effect on anyone with coeliac disease and avoiding gluten is crucial for sufferers of this disease. But coeliac disease isn't the only reason why many people are choosing to go gluten free. There are people who have a milder gluten intolerance and report feeling much better when following a gluten-free diet – experiencing improved stamina and energy levels.

The awareness and promotion in the media of the potential health benefits felt from following a gluten-free diet has increased dramatically over the past few years and the range and quality of meals and ingredients available have improved significantly. Gluten-free options in restaurants are now much more exciting than they were previously, and to make it easier, many restaurants now use coded symbols on menus to identify which meals are gluten free. Likewise, many supermarkets have now dedicated sections of the store to stocking gluten-free ingredients like flour and pasta, or ready-made products, providing a one-stop shop for picking up ingredients.

If you decide to go gluten free, understanding what foods and ingredients are going to cause problems is a good first step. Wheat, rye, barley and spelt are the obvious ones to avoid, and many baked goods, breakfast cereals, noodles and pasta will contain at least one of those grains. Couscous, bulgar wheat, semolina, farro, freekeh, khorasan and triticale all contain gluten as well as a few other more uncommon grains, so always check. Oats are gluten-free, but they contain a similar protein, and are often contaminated in facilities that process other grains, so always buy oats that are labelled gluten free.

Anything that is coated in batter or breadcrumbs must be avoided, and processed meats, such as sausages, often contain wheat or other grains. Sauces and condiments, such as soy sauce, mustard, and even tomato purée, may contain gluten, so always read the label and go for the gluten-free option. Ready-made stuffings and desserts can be problematic, and some yogurts may be thickened with wheat or gluten so always check. Beers, barley waters and malted milk must be avoided too. If you are in any doubt about a foodstuff or drink, don't buy it. You may come across products that are labelled 'wheat-free' – but this is no guarantee that they're gluten free. Whatever you're buying always read the label or get advice from a coeliac advice group about choosing suitable products.

People who have coeliac disease or severe gluten intolerance have to learn how to handle food and what precautions are worth taking to avoid any cross-contamination. If you share a kitchen with gluten-eaters, always make sure that all work surfaces, pots, pans and utensils are kept scrupulously clean. Don't share toasters, chopping boards, bread bins, biscuit tins, food processors or deep fryers with anyone who includes gluten in their diet, and always make sure that any food you keep in the fridge or food cupboard is well sealed. Be careful with jams or spreads that have been used on ordinary bread, in case any crumbs have been left in the jar.

While there are definitely ingredients to avoid you may be surprised by how many foods are naturally free from gluten. Things like fruit, vegetables, meat, fish and shellfish, poultry, dairy products, nuts, pulses and rice are staple ingredients that can be transformed into a huge array of dishes without the need for any gluten-free substitutes. Make the best of fresh, natural ingredients that can be enjoyed by everyone in the family.

There are, however, substitutes available in most supermarkets for all manner of ingredients, so you can still enjoy old favourites like pasta, noodles, bread and many more that have all been modified so they are gluten free. These ready-made ingredients can usually be treated in the same way you would use the ordinary versions. Gluten-free bread can be transformed into a healthy breakfast when topped with avocado in Smashed Avocado with Toasted Hemp Seeds (see page 35).

Or you can totally reimagine gluten-free ingredients and have a go at making fresh and healthy alternatives. By using strips of courgette to resemble spaghetti or noodles you get a quick and nutritious take on a classic ingredient – try them in Tamarind Turkey with Courgette Noodles (see page 142). Or whip up a quick couscous alternative by processing cauliflower florets in a food processor into couscous-like 'grains'.

For gluten-free baking, there are alternative bread or baked treats available to buy but it's much more satisfying to make your own. With a slightly different approach and some alternative flours and ingredients you can still produce bakes to be proud of at home. With a bit of practice you'll be whipping up delicious treats with confidence.

With all the delicious and innovative recipes for family meals in this book, no one will feel they're missing out, even if only one member of your family is gluten free. Get cooking!

CHAPTER ONE

BREAKFAST

BUCKWHEAT BREAKFAST BOWL

SERVES: *4* | **PREP:** *20–25 mins, plus soaking* | **COOK:** *No cooking*

INGREDIENTS

150 g/5½ oz buckwheat

500 ml/18 fl oz cold water

*400 g/14 oz plain dairy-free
  coconut yogurt*

grated zest and juice of 1 orange

3 tbsp goji berries

100 g/3½ oz raspberries

*1 Granny Smith apple, cored and
  diced*

1 tbsp pumpkin seeds

2 passion fruit, pulp only

2 tsp ground cinnamon

½ tsp ground turmeric

seeds from 1 pomegranate

2 tbsp agave syrup

1. Rinse the buckwheat three times in fresh water to clean the groats. Place in a bowl with the cold water and leave to soak for 30 minutes.

2. Drain and rinse the buckwheat and leave to stand at room temperature – in either a sprouting tray or a sieve with a bowl beneath – for 36 hours. Rinse the buckwheat if the groats look sticky, then rinse again before using.

3. Drain the buckwheat and divide between four bowls. Divide the yogurt between the bowls, then sprinkle over the remaining ingredients and serve.

PEAR, BANANA &
APPLE BREAKFAST BOWL

SERVES: *2* | **PREP:** *10 mins, plus optional chilling* | **COOK:** *No cooking*

INGREDIENTS

2 ripe dessert pears

*2 green-skinned apples, such as
Granny Smith*

*1 large banana, peeled and
chopped*

75 ml/2½ fl oz apple juice

juice of ½ lemon

2 tbsp sultanas

2 tbsp cashew nuts

1 tbsp sunflower seeds

1 tbsp sugar

½ tsp ground cinnamon

1 tbsp golden berries

1 tbsp cranberries

1. Core and chop one pear and one apple. Place them in a serving bowl with half the banana and pour over half the apple juice and half the lemon juice. Stir well to combine.

2. Core, peel and roughly chop the remaining pear and apple. Add to a blender with the rest of the banana.

3. Add the remaining apple juice and lemon juice to the blender with the sultanas and nuts and whizz until finely chopped.

4. Stir the blended mixture into the chopped fruit, along with the sunflower seeds, sugar and cinnamon. Scatter over the golden berries and cranberries. Chill in the refrigerator if you have time, or serve immediately.

QUINOA PORRIDGE WITH CARAMELIZED BANANA

SERVES: *2* | **PREP:** *5 mins* | **COOK:** *25 mins*

INGREDIENTS

400 ml/14 fl oz canned coconut
*   milk*
¼ tsp ground nutmeg
½ vanilla pod, split
100 g/3½ oz quinoa
1½ tbsp clear honey
1 large banana
25 g/1 oz unsalted butter
25 g/1 oz soft brown sugar
pinch of salt
25 g/1 oz coconut flakes, toasted
1 tbsp sesame seeds, toasted

1. Pour 300 ml/10 fl oz coconut milk into a medium saucepan over a low heat. Add the nutmeg and vanilla pod and bring to a simmer. Add the quinoa, bring to the boil and cook for 10–15 minutes.

2. Reduce the heat, stir through the honey and simmer for a further 5 minutes. Remove from the heat and take out the vanilla pod. Stir through the remaining milk, cover and leave to stand while you halve the banana lengthways, then halve again.

3. Place a medium-sized frying pan over a medium–high heat, add the butter, sugar and salt and heat until the mixture starts to foam. Add the sliced banana and fry it gently on both sides for 3–4 minutes, or until the banana starts to brown and become caramelized.

4. Spoon the porridge into two bowls and top with the banana, toasted coconut flakes and sesame seeds. Serve immediately.

BERRY CRUNCH

INGREDIENTS

75 g/2¾ oz rice, buckwheat or
*   millet flakes, or a mixture*
4 tbsp clear honey
500 g/1 lb 2 oz plain Greek strained
*   yogurt*
finely grated rind of 1 orange
225 g/8 oz frozen mixed berries,
*   partially thawed, plus extra to*
*   decorate*

1. Heat a dry frying pan over a medium heat, add the flakes and toast, shaking the pan, for 1 minute. Add half the honey and stir to coat the flakes. Cook, stirring constantly, until the flakes turn golden brown and slightly crisp.

2. Put the yogurt into a bowl and stir in the remaining honey and the orange rind. Gently stir in the berries, reserving a few to decorate. Leave to stand for 10–15 minutes so that the berries can release their juices, then stir again to give a swirl of colour.

3. To serve, spoon a layer of flakes into the bottom of four glasses, then top with a layer of the berry yogurt. Sprinkle with another layer of flakes and add another layer of the yogurt. Decorate with the reserved berries.

RAW CARROT, APPLE & GOJI BIRCHER MUESLI

SERVES: *4* | **PREP:** *15 mins, plus chilling* | **COOK:** *No cooking*

INGREDIENTS

125 g/4½ oz buckwheat flakes

1 carrot, grated

2 red-skinned apples

150 ml/5 fl oz apple juice

150 ml/5 fl oz almond milk

1½ tbsp dried goji berries

2 tbsp chopped hazelnuts

2 tbsp chopped dried apricots

1½ tbsp shelled pistachio nuts

1 tbsp sunflower seeds

1. Put the buckwheat flakes and carrot in a large bowl. Core, thinly slice and chop one of the apples and add to the bowl. Stir the bowl contents well until thoroughly combined. Stir in the apple juice, almond milk and 1 tablespoon of the goji berries. Cover and chill in the refrigerator overnight.

2. In the morning, stir the hazelnuts into the bowl. Core, thinly slice and chop the remaining apple.

3. Divide the muesli between four bowls and sprinkle over the apple, the remaining goji berries, apricots, pistachio nuts and sunflower seeds. Serve immediately.

VERY BERRY
OVERNIGHT OATS

SERVES: *1* | **PREP:** *5 mins, plus chilling* | **COOK:** *No cooking*

INGREDIENTS

40 g/1½ oz gluten-free rolled oats

½ tbsp milled linseeds

½ tbsp acai berry powder

2 tsp goji berries

1 tbsp flaked almonds

½ tbsp clear honey

125 ml/4 fl oz almond milk

2 blueberries

3 strawberries

1. Put the oats, linseeds, acai berry powder, goji berries, most of the flaked almonds, the honey and almond milk in a lidded 225–250-ml/8–9-fl oz jar. Stir well.

2. Stir a few of the blueberries into the oat mixture. Put the lid on the jar and chill in the refrigerator overnight.

3. In the morning, chop the strawberries. Top the oats with the remaining blueberries, strawberries and the remaining almonds.

MAPLE-BAKED OATS
WITH PLUMS

SERVES: 6 | **PREP:** *10 mins, plus soaking* | **COOK:** *35–40 mins*

INGREDIENTS

500 ml/18 fl oz semi-skimmed milk

2 eggs

35 g/1¼ oz unsalted butter, melted,
plus extra for greasing

60 g/2¼ oz dark brown sugar

75 ml/2½ fl oz maple syrup

4 ripe plums, stoned and cut into
8 pieces

1 large cooking apple, peeled and
cut into 1-cm/½-inch cubes

200 g/7 oz gluten-free rolled oats

1 tsp gluten-free baking powder

1 tsp cinnamon

pinch of salt

50 g/1¾ oz flaked almonds

1. Preheat the oven to 180°C/350°F/Gas Mark 4. Grease the base of a 2-litre/3½-pint ovenproof dish.

2. In a small bowl or jug, gently whisk together the milk, eggs, melted butter, 2 tablespoons of the sugar and the maple syrup.

3. Put half the plums, the apple cubes, oats, baking powder, cinnamon and salt into the prepared dish. Mix everything together using your hands or a large spoon.

4. Gently pour the milk mixture over the fruit mixture and leave to soak for a few minutes.

5. Sprinkle over the remaining plums, the almonds and the remaining sugar.

6. Bake in the preheated oven for 35–40 minutes until the milk has been fully absorbed. Serve warm.

BREAKFAST MUFFINS

MAKES: *12 muffins* | **PREP:** *20–25 mins* | **COOK:** *20 mins*

INGREDIENTS

*300 g/10½ oz gluten-free plain
   white flour blend*
4 tsp gluten-free baking powder
½ tsp xanthan gum
1 tsp ground mixed spice
140 g/5 oz light muscovado sugar
40 g/1½ oz sunflower seeds
175 g/6 oz carrots, grated
*finely grated rind and juice of
   1 small orange*
2 eggs, beaten
150 ml/5 fl oz milk
100 ml/3½ fl oz sunflower oil
1 tsp vanilla extract

1. Preheat the oven to 200°C/400°F/Gas Mark 6. Line a deep muffin tin with 12 paper cases.

2. Sift the flour, baking powder, xanthan gum and mixed spice into a large bowl. Stir in the sugar with 25 g/1 oz of the sunflower seeds, the carrots and orange rind.

3. Lightly beat together the orange juice, eggs, milk, oil and vanilla with a fork and stir into the dry ingredients, mixing to a rough batter.

4. Spoon the batter into the prepared tin and sprinkle with the remaining sunflower seeds. Bake in the preheated oven for about 20 minutes, or until well risen and golden brown. Serve warm.

PEACHY TOFU FOOL

SERVES: *4* | **PREP:** *20–25 mins* | **COOK:** *No cooking*

INGREDIENTS

4 peaches or nectarines, stoned

3 tbsp orange juice

350 g/12 oz pack soft silken tofu,
*   drained*

2 tbsp maple syrup

40 g/1½ oz walnut pieces, roughly
*   chopped*

1 tbsp demerara sugar

1. Roughly chop the peaches and purée with a hand blender or in a food processor until smooth. Add the orange juice and blend again.

2. Whizz the tofu with a hand blender or in a food processor until smooth. Stir in the maple syrup.

3. Place alternate tablespoons of the fruit purée and tofu mixture in four tall glasses or individual dishes, lightly swirling together for a marbled effect.

4. Mix the walnuts and sugar together, and spoon on top of the fools just before serving.

FLUFFY PANCAKES WITH BLUEBERRIES & ALMONDS

MAKES: *12–14 pancakes* | **PREP:** *20 mins* | **COOK:** *15 mins*

INGREDIENTS

5 eggs, separated
175 g/6 oz gluten-free plain flour
1½ tsp gluten-free baking powder
pinch of salt
150 ml/5 fl oz semi-skimmed milk
olive oil, for frying

TO SERVE

70 g/2½ oz toasted flaked almonds
50 ml/2 fl oz agave syrup
100 g/3½ oz blueberries

1. Mix the egg yolks with the flour, baking powder and salt, then stir in the milk.

2. Whisk the egg whites and delicately fold them into the mixture until combined.

3. Heat some oil in a heavy-based frying pan, then drop in spoonfuls of the batter. Cook for about 1 minute, or until bubbles start to form, then turn over with a spatula and cook on the other side. Remove the pancakes from the pan and keep them warm in the oven until ready to serve.

4. Serve the pancakes warm, topped with the almonds, agave syrup and blueberries.

BANANA CRÊPES

SERVES: *4* | **PREP:** *20–25 mins, plus resting* | **COOK:** *30 mins*

INGREDIENTS

50 g/1¾ oz buckwheat flour
50 g/1¾ oz gluten-free plain flour
pinch of salt
1 large egg, lightly beaten
125 ml/4 fl oz milk
125 ml/4 fl oz water
40 g/1½ oz butter or margarine

MAPLE SYRUP BANANAS

40 g/1½ oz butter or margarine
2 tbsp maple syrup
2 bananas, thickly sliced on the
  diagonal

1. Sift together the buckwheat flour, plain flour and salt into a mixing bowl. Make a well in the centre and add the beaten egg, milk and water. Using a balloon whisk, gradually mix the flour into the liquid ingredients. Whisk until you have a smooth batter.

2. Melt 25 g/1 oz of the butter in a small saucepan and stir into the batter. Pour the batter into a jug, cover and leave to rest for 30 minutes.

3. Melt half the remaining butter in a medium-sized frying pan. When the pan is hot, pour in enough batter to make a thin crêpe, swirling the pan to achieve an even layer.

4. Cook one side until lightly browned, then, using a palette knife, turn over and cook the other side. Slide onto a warmed plate and cover with foil while you cook the remaining crêpes, adding more butter when needed.

5. To make the maple syrup bananas, wipe out the pan, add the butter and heat until melted. Stir in the maple syrup, then add the bananas and cook for 2–3 minutes, or until the bananas have just softened and the sauce has thickened and caramelized. To serve, fold the crêpes in half and half again, then top with the bananas.

COCOA WAFFLES
WITH RASPBERRIES

SERVES: *6* | **PREP:** *20 mins* | **COOK:** *15–30 mins*

INGREDIENTS

5 large eggs, separated

pinch of salt

1 tbsp pure dark cocoa powder

40 g/1½ oz caster sugar

50 g/1¾ oz unsalted butter, melted and cooled slightly

250 ml/9 fl oz semi-skimmed milk

225 g/8 oz gluten-free plain flour

olive oil, for brushing

TO SERVE

150 g/5½ oz plain Greek strained yogurt

200 g/7 oz fresh raspberries

6 tbsp clear honey

1. You will need a waffle maker for this recipe. Place the egg yolks, salt, cocoa powder and sugar in a medium-sized bowl and beat well with a wooden spoon. Stir in the butter. Slowly beat in the milk until fully incorporated. Gradually add the flour until a thick batter forms.

2. In a separate bowl, whisk the egg whites until stiff peaks hold, then gently fold them into the batter. Gently combine the mixture.

3. Heat the waffle maker according to manufacturer's instructions. Brush with the oil and spoon the mixture in. Do not overfill. Cook for 4–5 minutes and serve topped with yogurt, raspberries and honey.

MATCHA
POWER SMOOTHIE

SERVES: *1* | **PREP:** *5 mins, plus optional chilling* | **COOK:** *No cooking*

INGREDIENTS

25 g/1 oz spinach

1 banana, peeled and chopped

1 small ripe avocado, peeled,
stoned and roughly chopped

2 kiwi fruits, peeled and sliced

125 ml/4 fl oz almond milk

½ tbsp clear honey

1 tsp matcha tea powder

½ tsp gluten-free wheatgrass
powder

2 tsp flaked almonds, to decorate

½ tsp maca powder, to decorate

1. Purée the spinach, banana, avocado and one of the kiwi fruits in a blender with half the milk.

2. Add the honey, matcha, wheatgrass and the remaining milk to the blender and blend until smooth. Pour the smoothie into a bowl. Chill for 1 hour if you have time.

3. Top with the remaining kiwi fruit and decorate with the flaked almonds and maca powder.

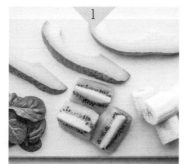

VANILLA, ALMOND & BANANA SMOOTHIE

SERVES: 2 | **PREP:** 5 mins | **COOK:** No cooking

INGREDIENTS

225 ml/8 fl oz almond milk
60 g/2¼ oz almond butter
1 banana, sliced
4 stoned dates
1 tsp vanilla extract
8–10 ice cubes

1. Place the almond milk, almond butter, banana, dates, vanilla extract and ice cubes in a blender.

2. Blend on high speed until smooth.

3. Pour into two glasses and serve immediately.

SPICY BLACK BEAN & SWEETCORN SCRAMBLE WITH TOASTED POLENTA

SERVES: *2* | **PREP:** *20 mins, plus chilling* | **COOK:** *20 mins*

INGREDIENTS
TOASTED POLENTA

70 g/2½ oz fine yellow cornmeal
375 ml/13 fl oz water
1 tsp gluten-free vegetable bouillon
*   powder*
1 tbsp nutritional yeast flakes
½ tsp sea salt
extra virgin rapeseed oil, for
*   brushing*

BLACK BEAN & SWEETCORN SCRAMBLE

1 tbsp extra virgin rapeseed oil
25 g/1 oz finely chopped red onion
25 g/1 oz finely chopped sweet red
*   pepper*
1 small garlic clove, crushed
3 tbsp sweetcorn kernels, cooked
*   and rinsed*
3 tbsp black beans, cooked and
*   rinsed*
1 tsp gluten-free chilli sauce
4 eggs, beaten

1. Line a 15-cm/6-inch square shallow dish or baking tray with baking paper.

2. Put the cornmeal in a small jug. Bring the water to the boil in a saucepan with the bouillon powder and, when it is boiling fast, gradually pour in the cornmeal, stirring constantly. Continue to cook over a high heat for 3 minutes, stirring until it thickens. Reduce the heat, stir in the yeast and salt and simmer, stirring frequently, until you have a fairly thick paste.

3. Spoon the cornmeal mixture into the prepared dish. Cover with clingfilm or foil and place in the refrigerator for 2 hours, or until quite firm. Cut into four triangles.

4. To make the scramble, add half the oil to a small frying pan and place over a medium heat. Add the onion and red pepper and cook for 7 minutes, or until soft. Stir in the garlic, sweetcorn, beans and chilli sauce and cook for a further 1 minute. Set aside and keep warm until ready to serve.

5. Preheat a ridged griddle pan or the grill to medium. Lightly brush the polenta triangles with oil and cook until turning golden and flecked dark brown. Turn and cook on the other side.

6. Add the remaining oil to a separate small frying pan and place over a medium heat. Add the eggs and cook, stirring occasionally with a spatula or wooden spoon until lightly scrambled. Gently stir the bean mixture into the eggs and serve with the toasted polenta.

SMASHED AVOCADO WITH TOASTED HEMP SEEDS

SERVES: *2* | **PREP:** *10 mins* | **COOK:** *5–6 mins*

INGREDIENTS

2 tbsp hemp seeds

2 ripe avocados, roughly chopped

1 tbsp lemon juice

½ tbsp extra virgin olive oil

1 large garlic clove, crushed

½ tsp sea salt

½ tsp pepper

2 thick slices gluten-free wholegrain bread

½ fresh red chilli, deseeded and finely chopped, to garnish

1. Place a small, non-stick frying pan over a medium heat. Add the hemp seeds and toast them for 1–2 minutes, then set aside in a small dish until needed.

2. Place the avocado in a large bowl. Add the lemon juice, oil, garlic, salt, pepper and 1½ tbsp of the toasted hemp seeds. Stir to combine, then mash to a rough purée.

3. Toast the wholegrain bread and serve the purée on the toast, sprinkled with the remaining hemp seeds and the chopped chilli.

SAUSAGE &
EGG SIZZLE

SERVES: *4* | **PREP:** *20 mins* | **COOK:** *35–40 mins*

INGREDIENTS

4 gluten-free sausages

sunflower oil, for frying

*4 peeled, boiled potatoes, cooled
    and diced*

8 cherry tomatoes

4 eggs, beaten

salt and pepper (optional)

1. Preheat the grill to medium–high. Arrange the sausages on a foil-lined grill pan and cook under the preheated grill, turning occasionally, for 12–15 minutes, or until cooked through and golden brown. Leave to cool slightly, then cut into bite-sized pieces.

2. Meanwhile, heat a little oil in a 25-cm/10-inch heavy-based frying pan with a heatproof handle over a medium heat. Add the potatoes and cook until golden brown and crisp all over, then add the tomatoes and cook for a further 2 minutes. Arrange the sausages in the pan so that there is an even distribution of potatoes, tomatoes and sausages.

3. Add a little more oil to the pan if it seems dry. Season the beaten eggs with salt and pepper to taste, if using, and pour the mixture over the ingredients in the pan. Cook for 3 minutes, without stirring or disturbing the eggs. Place the pan under the preheated grill for 3 minutes, or until the top is just cooked. Cut into wedges to serve.

POTATO & ONION FRITTATA

SERVES: *4* | **PREP:** *15 mins* | **COOK:** *1 hour*

INGREDIENTS

4 tbsp olive oil

2 large onions, halved and thinly sliced

125 ml/4 fl oz water

50 g/1¾ oz red quinoa, rinsed

700 g/1 lb 9 oz waxy potatoes, peeled, halved lengthways and thinly sliced

9 eggs

½ tsp dried oregano

½ tsp salt

½ tsp pepper

1. Heat the oil in a frying pan, add the onions and gently fry over a low–medium heat for 25 minutes until golden and very soft. Drain the onions, reserving the oil.

2. Meanwhile, put the water and quinoa into a small saucepan and bring to the boil. Cover and simmer over a very low heat for 10 minutes, or until most of the liquid has evaporated. Remove from the heat, but leave the pan covered for a further 10 minutes to allow the grains to swell. Fluff up with a fork.

3. Meanwhile, put the potatoes in a steamer and steam for 8 minutes, or until just tender. Spread out on a clean tea towel to dry.

4. Beat the eggs with the oregano, salt and pepper. Stir the onions, potatoes and quinoa into the egg mixture.

5. Preheat the grill to medium–high. Heat the reserved oil in a deep 25-cm/10-inch non-stick frying pan with a heatproof handle. Pour in the egg mixture, cover and cook over a low–medium heat for 15 minutes. Place the pan under the preheated grill for 5 minutes to finish cooking the top of the frittata.

6. Turn out onto a plate, cut into wedges and serve immediately.

POTATO CAKES

SERVES: *4* | **PREP:** *20 mins* | **COOK:** *20–25 mins*

INGREDIENTS

115 g/4 oz cold home-made
  mashed potatoes
200 ml/7 fl oz milk
75 g/2¾ oz gluten-free self-raising
  flour
pinch of salt
1 egg, beaten
sunflower oil, for frying

TO SERVE

8 good-quality bacon rashers,
  grilled until crisp
1½ tbsp maple syrup

1. Put the mashed potatoes and milk in a food processor or blender and process to a thin purée.

2. Sift together the flour and salt into a mixing bowl, make a well in the centre and add the beaten egg and potato purée. Using a balloon whisk, gradually mix the flour into the liquid ingredients, whisking to a smooth, creamy, fairly thick batter.

3. Heat a little oil in a large, non-stick frying pan. Pour 1 tablespoon of batter per cake into the pan – you will probably fit about three in the pan at one time. Cook each cake for 2 minutes on each side until golden brown. Remove from the pan and keep warm while you cook the remaining potato cakes.

4. Divide the cakes between 4 warmed plates, top each serving with 2 bacon rashers and drizzle with maple syrup.

POACHED EGGS WITH
TOMATO & RED PEPPER

SERVES: *3-4* | **PREP:** *20 mins* | **COOK:** *30–35 mins*

INGREDIENTS

2 tbsp olive oil

1 red chilli, deseeded and finely chopped

1 onion, finely chopped

3 red peppers, deseeded and sliced into thin strips

4 garlic cloves, roughly chopped

1 tsp ground cumin

1 tsp ground turmeric

¼ tsp saffron

400 g/14 oz canned chopped tomatoes

3 eggs

2 tbsp roughly chopped fresh flat-leaf parsley, to garnish

4 tbsp natural yogurt, to serve

1. In a deep frying pan with a lid, heat the oil until hot, then add the red chilli and onion. Sizzle for 2–3 minutes until the onion has begun to soften. Add the red peppers, garlic, cumin, turmeric and saffron and fry, covered, for 10–12 minutes until the peppers are soft but not charred.

2. Add the tomatoes to the pan and simmer for a further 8 minutes, uncovered, until the mixture has thickened slightly.

3. Using a spoon, shape three holes in the pepper mixture and crack an egg into each hole (if using a smaller pan, create one hole and use a single egg per serving). The white may seep onto the surface of the mixture. Cover the pan and cook for about 10 minutes until the yolks are just set.

4. Serve immediately, with a sprinkling of parsley and some yogurt.

CHAPTER TWO

SIDES &
SNACKS

ONION & ROOT VEGETABLE WINTER ROAST

SERVES: *4* | **PREP:** *15 mins* | **COOK:** *45 mins*

INGREDIENTS

2 red onions, quartered, about 200 g/7 oz total weight
6 small shallots
200 g/7 oz parsnips, cut into thick batons
200 g/7 oz sweet potatoes, cut into thick batons
200 g/7 oz yams, cut into thick batons
150 g/5½ oz Jerusalem artichokes, scrubbed and halved
8 large garlic cloves, unpeeled
1 tbsp rapeseed oil
1 tbsp lemon juice
1 tsp salt
pepper (optional)

1. Preheat the oven to 190°C/375°F/Gas Mark 5. Place the onions and shallots in a roasting tin.

2. Add the parsnips, sweet potatoes, yams, Jerusalem artichokes and garlic to the tin.

3. Pour in the oil and lemon juice. Add the salt with pepper to taste, if using, then stir so that the vegetables are thoroughly coated with the oil and lemon juice.

4. Bake in the preheated oven for 20 minutes. Turn the vegetables with a spatula and bake for a further 25 minutes, or until golden and cooked through. The garlic cloves should be meltingly soft inside – if you like, press the contents of each garlic clove into the pan juices and stir in with a little water. Serve immediately.

POTATO SALAD

SERVES: *4* | **PREP:** *5–10 mins, plus standing* | **COOK:** *25–30 mins*

INGREDIENTS

500 g/1 lb 2 oz new potatoes,
*   unpeeled*
5 spring onions
1 handful fresh mint leaves
1 handful fresh parsley
salt (optional)

DRESSING

4 tbsp extra virgin rapeseed oil
1 tbsp white wine vinegar
1 tsp caster sugar
1 tsp gluten-free French mustard
salt and pepper (optional)

1. Put the potatoes in a saucepan, cover with water, add a little salt, if using, and place over a medium–high heat. Bring to the boil and simmer for about 20 minutes, or until the potatoes are tender.

2. Meanwhile, slice the spring onions, retaining most of the green parts, and finely chop the mint and parsley. Put the oil, vinegar, sugar, mustard, and salt and pepper, if using, into a bowl and mix well together.

3. Drain the potatoes and return them in the pan to the hot hob (switched off) for 1 minute to evaporate any remaining moisture.

4. While the potatoes are still hot, tip them into a bowl and roughly chop. Add the spring onions, herbs and dressing and stir to mix thoroughly. Cover and leave to stand for 1 hour before serving so that the potatoes can absorb the oil and flavourings.

TOMATO FOCACCIA

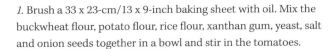

MAKES: *1 loaf* | **PREP:** *25 mins, plus rising and cooling* | **COOK:** *25–30 mins*

INGREDIENTS

*3 tbsp olive oil, plus extra for
    brushing*
200 g/7 oz buckwheat flour
200 g/7 oz potato flour
200 g/7 oz rice flour
2 tsp xanthan gum
*7 g/1⁄3 oz sachet gluten-free fast-
    action yeast*
1½ tsp salt
½ tsp black onion seeds
*40 g/1½ oz sun-dried tomatoes,
    soaked, drained and chopped*
600 ml/1 pint lukewarm water
1 small egg, beaten
2 garlic cloves, cut into slivers
a few fresh oregano sprigs

1. Brush a 33 x 23-cm/13 x 9-inch baking sheet with oil. Mix the buckwheat flour, potato flour, rice flour, xanthan gum, yeast, salt and onion seeds together in a bowl and stir in the tomatoes.

2. Make a well in the centre and stir in the water, egg and 1 tablespoon of the oil to make a very soft dough. Beat hard with a wooden spoon for 4–5 minutes, then spoon onto the prepared baking sheet, spreading evenly with a palette knife.

3. Cover with oiled clingfilm and leave to stand in a warm place for about 1 hour, or until doubled in size. Preheat the oven to 220°C/425°F/Gas Mark 7.

4. Press pieces of garlic and oregano into the dough at intervals. Drizzle with the remaining oil, then bake in the oven for 25–30 minutes, or until firm and golden brown. Transfer to a wire rack and leave to cool.

BUCKWHEAT FLATBREADS

SERVES: *4* | **PREP:** *20 mins* | **COOK:** *5 mins*

INGREDIENTS

*200 g/7 oz buckwheat flour, plus
   extra for dusting*
100 g/3½ oz rice flour
1 tsp salt
1 tsp gluten-free baking powder
½ tsp ground cumin
2 tbsp chopped fresh coriander
200 ml/7 fl oz water
2 tbsp olive oil

1. Sift together the buckwheat flour, rice flour, salt, baking powder and cumin into a large bowl and make a well in the centre.

2. Add the coriander, water and oil and stir into the dry ingredients to make a soft dough.

3. Divide the dough into four pieces and shape each piece into a smooth ball. Roll out each ball on a lightly floured work surface to a 20-cm/8-inch round.

4. Preheat a griddle pan or barbecue to very hot. Add the flatbreads and cook for about 1 minute on each side, or until firm and golden brown. Serve warm.

RED CABBAGE SALAD
WITH AUBERGINE DIP

SERVES: *4* | **PREP:** *10–15 mins* | **COOK:** *15–20 mins*

INGREDIENTS

2 carrots

350 g/12 oz red cabbage, shredded

55 g/2 oz raisins

125 g/4½ oz bistro salad (a mix of
red-stemmed baby red chard,
bull's blood chard and lamb's
lettuce)

juice of 1 orange

pepper (optional)

DIP

3 aubergines

3 garlic cloves, finely chopped

2 tbsp gluten-free tahini

3 tbsp hemp oil

pepper (optional)

1. To make the dip, preheat the grill to high and remove the grill rack. Prick both ends of each aubergine with a fork, put them in the grill pan and grill 5 cm/2 inches away from the heat source, turning several times, for 15–20 minutes until blackened. Leave to cool.

2. Shave the carrots into long, thin ribbons using a swivel-bladed vegetable peeler, then put them on a serving plate. Add the cabbage, then sprinkle over the raisins and salad leaves. Drizzle with the orange juice and season with a little pepper, if using.

3. Cut the aubergines in half and scoop the soft flesh away from the blackened skins using a dessertspoon. Finely chop the flesh, then put it in a bowl. Add the garlic, tahini and hemp oil, season with a little pepper, if using, and mix together. Spoon into a serving bowl and nestle in the centre of the salad to serve.

JEWEL SALAD WITH RANCH DRESSING

SERVES: *4* | **PREP:** *20 mins, plus soaking* | **COOK:** *No cooking*

INGREDIENTS

2 large tomatoes, deseeded

1 cucumber

½ red onion

1 carrot

1 yellow pepper, deseeded

10 red radishes

8 tbsp mixed chopped fresh
herbs, such as parsley, mint and
coriander

zest and juice of ½ lemon

4 tbsp cold-pressed extra virgin
olive oil

½ tsp sea salt

½ tsp black pepper

RANCH DRESSING

100 g/3½ oz unsalted cashew nuts,
soaked in water for 2 hours,
drained and rinsed

1 tbsp cider vinegar

125 ml/4 fl oz coconut milk

1 garlic clove, crushed

½ tsp sea salt

2 spring onions, finely chopped

2 tbsp chopped fresh parsley

1. To make the dressing, put the soaked nuts, vinegar, 50 ml/ 2 fl oz of the coconut milk, the garlic and salt in a blender and blend to a smooth paste. Gradually add the remaining coconut milk until the mixture is fairly thick. The consistency should be between pouring and a dip.

2. Stir in the spring onions and parsley.

3. To make the salad, finely chop the vegetables and put them in a large serving bowl or four individual bowls. Stir in all the remaining salad ingredients and serve.

FRISÉE SALAD WITH WALNUT DRESSING

SERVES: *4* | **PREP:** *10 mins* | **COOK:** *5 mins, plus cooling*

INGREDIENTS

½ head of frisée lettuce, leaves
separated and torn into bite-
sized pieces
1 cos lettuce heart, leaves separated
and torn into bite-sized pieces

DRESSING

55 g/2 oz walnut pieces, larger
pieces broken up
3 tbsp olive oil
1 tsp clear honey
1 tbsp white wine vinegar
1 tsp gluten-free Dijon mustard
¼ tsp pepper

1. To make the dressing, put the walnuts in a frying pan, add 1 tablespoon of the oil and cook over a medium heat for 2–3 minutes, or until lightly toasted. Remove from the heat, drizzle over the honey and stir. The heat from the pan will be enough to caramelize the mixture slightly.

2. Add the remaining oil, stir, then leave to cool for 15 minutes so the walnuts flavour the oil. Put the vinegar and mustard in a small bowl, season with the pepper and beat together. Stir this into the cooled walnuts and oil.

3. Put the lettuce leaves in a salad bowl. Spoon over the walnut dressing, gently toss together and serve.

INDIAN SPICED SLAW

SERVES: *4* | **PREP:** *20 mins* | **COOK:** *5 mins*

INGREDIENTS

175 g/6 oz red cabbage, shredded
40 g/1½ oz kale, shredded
1 red apple, cored and coarsely
  grated
1 large carrot, coarsely grated

TOPPING

2 tbsp pumpkin seeds
2 tbsp sunflower seeds
2 tbsp flaked almonds
½ tsp gluten-free garam masala
¼ tsp ground turmeric
1 tbsp sunflower oil

DRESSING

150 g/5½ oz natural yogurt
1 tsp gluten-free garam masala
¼ tsp ground turmeric
salt and pepper (optional)

1. To make the topping, heat a frying pan over a medium heat. Put the pumpkin seeds, sunflower seeds, almonds, garam masala and turmeric in the hot pan and add the oil. Cook for 3–4 minutes, stirring frequently, until the almonds are golden-brown. Remove from the heat and leave to cool.

2. Meanwhile, to make the dressing, put the yogurt, garam masala and turmeric in a large bowl, then season to taste with salt and pepper, if using, and stir well.

3. Add the cabbage, kale, apple and carrot to the bowl and gently toss. Divide the salad between four bowls, sprinkle over the topping and serve.

SPICED RED CABBAGE &
CORIANDER CROQUETTES

MAKES: *8 croquettes* | **PREP:** *30 mins, plus chilling* | **COOK:** *30–45 mins*

INGREDIENTS

400 g/14 oz white potatoes, peeled
  and cut into chunks
½ small red cabbage, shredded
2 tbsp olive oil
1 tsp cumin seeds
1 red onion, finely chopped
1 garlic clove, crushed
2 egg yolks
1 tsp ground turmeric
½ tsp hot chilli powder
½ tsp ground coriander
15 g/½ oz fresh coriander, roughly
  chopped
25 g/1 oz gluten-free plain flour
2 tbsp sunflower oil
salt and pepper (optional)

1. Bring a large saucepan of water to the boil over a high heat. Add the potatoes, reduce the heat to simmering and cook for 15–20 minutes. Drain and leave to steam dry.

2. Bring a medium-sized sauce pan of water to the boil. Add the red cabbage and cook over a medium heat for 5–10 minutes, or until tender. Drain well and toss in 1 tablespoon of the olive oil and the cumin seeds.

3. Heat the remaining olive oil in a small saucepan over a low heat. Add the onion and gently cook for 5–10 minutes, or until it begins to soften. Add the garlic and cook for a further 3 minutes. Set aside until needed.

4. Roughly mash the potatoes, leaving some lumps. Stir through the egg yolks, turmeric, chilli powder, ground coriander, onion mixture and cabbage, then stir in the fresh coriander. Season to taste with salt and pepper, if using.

5. Shape the mixture into 8 patties and chill in the refrigerator for at least 30 minutes.

6. Lightly coat each croquette in the flour, shaking off any excess. Heat the sunflower oil in a large, heavy-based frying pan over a medium–high heat. Add the croquettes and cook for 5 minutes on each side until crisp and golden brown. Serve immediately.

VEGETABLE PAKORAS

SERVES: *4* | **PREP:** *30–40 mins* | **COOK:** *20 mins*

INGREDIENTS

6 tbsp gram flour

½ tsp salt

1 tsp chilli powder

1 tsp gluten-free baking powder

1½ tsp white cumin seeds

1 tsp pomegranate seeds

300 ml/10 fl oz water

*¼ bunch of fresh coriander, finely
    chopped*

*400 g/14 oz mixed vegetables of
    your choice: cauliflower, cut into
    small florets; onions, cut into
    rings and potatoes, sliced*

vegetable oil, for deep frying

2 fresh coriander sprigs, to garnish

1. Sift the flour into a large bowl. Add the salt, chilli powder, baking powder, cumin seeds and pomegranate seeds and blend well together. Pour in the water and beat well until a smooth batter forms. Add the chopped coriander and mix well.

2. Dip the prepared vegetables into the batter, carefully shaking off any excess.

3. Heat enough oil for deep-frying in a wok, deep fryer or large, heavy-based saucepan to 180–190°C/350–375°F, or until a cube of bread browns in 30 seconds. Using tongs, place the battered vegetables in the oil and deep-fry, in batches, turning once.

4. Repeat this process until all of the batter has been used up. Transfer the fried vegetables to crumpled kitchen paper and drain thoroughly. Garnish with coriander sprigs and serve immediately.

SPRING ROLLS

MAKES: *16 spring rolls* | **PREP:** *25–30 mins, plus marinating* | **COOK:** *15–20 mins*

INGREDIENTS

2 tbsp gluten-free tamari

1½ tsp maple syrup

500 g/1 lb 2 oz lean pork fillets

vegetable oil, for frying

32 rice paper pancakes

6 tbsp gluten-free hoisin sauce, plus
*   extra to serve (optional)*

70 g/2½ oz rice vermicelli noodles,
*   cooked*

200 g/7 oz cucumber, sliced into
*   thin strips*

6 spring onions, sliced into thin
*   strips*

1. Blend the tamari and maple syrup together in a shallow dish. Add the pork and turn to coat in the mixture. Cover and leave to marinate in the refrigerator for at least 1 hour or overnight.

2. Heat a griddle pan over a medium–high heat until hot, add a little oil to cover the base, then add the pork and cook for 4–6 minutes on each side, depending on the thickness of the fillets, until cooked through and caramelized on the outside. Remove from the pan and slice into fine strips.

3. Fill a heatproof bowl with water that is just off the boil. Put two rice paper pancakes on top of one another (you will need two per roll as they are very thin and fragile) and soak in the water for 20 seconds, or until they become pliable and opaque. Carefully remove from the bowl with a spatula, drain and place flat on a plate.

4. Spread a spoonful of hoisin sauce over each pair of pancakes and top with a small bundle of noodles and a few strips of pork, cucumber and spring onion. Fold in the ends and sides of the pancake to resemble a spring roll. Set aside while you make the remaining rolls. Slice in half on the diagonal and serve with a little more hoisin sauce, if using.

HOT SALAMI & QUINOA BITES WITH GARLIC MAYO

MAKES: *15–20 bites* | **PREP:** *25 mins* | **COOK:** *20 mins*

INGREDIENTS

500 g/1 lb 2 oz cooked quinoa
50 g/1¾ oz gluten-free plain flour
50 g/1¾ oz sun-dried tomatoes,
  roughly chopped
3 tbsp chopped fresh parsley
25 g/1 oz freshly grated Parmesan
  cheese
2 eggs, lightly beaten
3 tbsp sunflower oil, for oiling
6 thin slices gluten-free salami, cut
  into strips
salt and pepper (optional)

GARLIC MAYONNAISE

70 g/2½ oz gluten-free mayonnaise
½ tsp smoked paprika
1 garlic clove, crushed

1. To make the garlic mayonnaise, combine the mayonnaise, paprika and garlic in a small bowl and set aside.

2. Line a baking tray with baking paper. Put the quinoa, flour, sun-dried tomatoes, 2 tablespoons of the parsley and the cheese in a large bowl and combine with the beaten eggs. Season to taste with salt and pepper, if using.

3. Shape the mixture into 15–20 small patties with your hands, then place on the prepared tray.

4. Heat the sunflower oil in a large non-stick frying pan. Add the patties in batches and cook on each side for 3–5 minutes, or until golden brown. Leave to rest on a tray lined with kitchen paper.

5. In the same pan, fry the salami until crisp and beginning to curl.

6. Serve the quinoa bites topped with ½ teaspoon of the garlic mayonnaise, the salami and any remaining parsley.

SWEET POTATO ROUNDS WITH GOAT'S CHEESE & OLIVES

MAKES: *15–20 rounds* | **PREP:** *20 mins* | **COOK:** *25–30 mins*

INGREDIENTS

olive oil, for oiling

2 large sweet potatoes, peeled and cut into 1-cm/½-inch slices

1 tbsp chilli oil

100 g/3½ oz goat's cheese, crumbled

100 g/3½ oz black olives, stoned and sliced

1 tbsp snipped fresh chives

salt and pepper (optional)

1. Preheat the oven to 200°C/400°F/Gas Mark 6. Oil a baking sheet with olive oil.

2. Place the potato slices on the prepared baking sheet and brush with chilli oil. Season to taste with salt and pepper, if using, and bake in the preheated oven for 20–25 minutes, turning halfway through, until the slices become crisp around the edges. Remove from the oven and reduce the oven temperature to 180°C/350°F/Gas Mark 4.

3. Sprinkle the rounds with the cheese and gently push the olives into the cheese. Return to the oven and cook for a further 5 minutes.

4. Garnish with the chives and serve.

ROAST KALE CRISPS

SERVES: *4* | **PREP:** *15 mins* | **COOK:** *15 mins*

INGREDIENTS

250 g/9 oz kale
2 tbsp olive oil
2 pinches of sugar
2 pinches of sea salt
2 tbsp toasted flaked almonds, to
*   garnish*

1. Preheat the oven to 150°C/300°F/Gas Mark 2. Remove the thick stems and central rib from the kale (leaving about 125 g/4½ oz trimmed leaves). Rinse and dry very thoroughly with kitchen paper. Tear into bite-sized pieces and place in a bowl with the oil and sugar, then toss well.

2. Spread about half the leaves in a single layer in a large roasting tin, spaced well apart. Sprinkle with a pinch of sea salt and roast on the bottom rack of the preheated oven for 4 minutes.

3. Stir the leaves, then turn the tray so the back is at the front. Roast for a further 1–2 minutes until the leaves are crisp and very slightly browned at the edges. Repeat with the remaining leaves and sea salt. Sprinkle the crisps with the flaked almonds and serve immediately.

CARROT & CASHEW PÂTÉ ON CRACKERS

SERVES: 4 | **PREP:** 5 mins, plus chilling | **COOK:** No cooking

INGREDIENTS

140 g/5 oz cashew nuts, soaked in
   cold water for at least 4 hours, or
   overnight
300 g/10½ oz carrots, chopped
55 g/2 oz light gluten-free tahini
juice of 1 lemon
2 tsp finely chopped fresh ginger
1 large garlic clove, crushed
½ tsp sea salt
2 tbsp chopped fresh coriander
   leaves
8 gluten-free mixed seed crackers
micro salad leaves, to serve

1. Drain the cashew nuts thoroughly.

2. Place all of the ingredients, except the coriander, in a food processor or blender and process until smooth.

3. Stir the coriander leaves into the mixture and spoon into four 8-cm/3¼-inch round ramekins. Cover with clingfilm and chill in the refrigerator for 2 hours.

4. Spread the pâté on the crackers and serve immediately with micro salad leaves.

TOMATO &
BEAN SALSA

SERVES: 4 | **PREP:** 20-25 mins, plus chilling & cooling | **COOK:** 5-10 mins

INGREDIENTS

200 g/7 oz cherry tomatoes,
quartered
1 small red onion, very finely
chopped
200 g/7 oz canned aduki beans,
drained and rinsed
½ red pepper, deseeded and finely
chopped
½–1 red chilli, deseeded and very
finely chopped
2 tsp gluten-free sun-dried tomato
purée
1 tsp agave nectar
large handful of chopped fresh
coriander
salt and pepper (optional)

1. Place the tomatoes, onion, beans, red pepper, chilli, tomato purée, agave nectar and coriander in a large bowl. Mix together well and season to taste with salt and pepper, if using.

2. Cover the bowl and chill in the refrigerator for at least 15 minutes to allow the flavours to develop. Preheat the grill to medium.

3. Place the tortillas under the preheated grill and lightly toast. Leave to cool slightly, then cut into slices.

4. Transfer the bean dip to a small bowl and serve.

SALMON DEVILLED EGGS WITH BLACK ONION SEEDS

MAKES: *16 halves* | **PREP:** *15 mins* | **COOK:** *8 mins*

INGREDIENTS

8 large eggs

50 ml/2 fl oz gluten-free mayonnaise

50 ml/2 fl oz crème fraîche

2 tsp gluten-free Dijon mustard

40 g/1½ oz smoked salmon, cut into small pieces

15 g/½ oz fresh dill, chopped

1 tbsp black onion seeds

salt and pepper (optional)

1. Put the eggs into a large saucepan and cover with cold water. Bring to the boil over a high heat, then reduce to a simmer and cook for 8 minutes. Drain and immediately refresh in cold water until cool.

2. Peel the eggs and cut in half. Scoop out the yolk and combine in a bowl with the mayonnaise, crème fraîche, mustard, salmon and half the dill. Season to taste with salt and pepper, if using.

3. Spoon the yolk mixture into the egg whites and serve topped with the remaining dill and the onion seeds.

SPICED BEETROOT & CUCUMBER TZATZIKI

SERVES: *4* | **PREP:** *10–15 mins* | **COOK:** *No cooking*

INGREDIENTS

*115 g/4 oz cooked beetroot in
natural juices, drained and diced
(drained weight)*
150 g/5½ oz cucumber, diced
40 g/1½ oz radishes, diced
1 spring onion, finely chopped
12 Little Gem lettuce leaves

DRESSING

*150 g/5½ oz plain Greek strained
yogurt*
¼ tsp ground cumin
½ tsp clear honey
2 tbsp finely chopped fresh mint
salt and pepper (optional)

1. To make the dressing, put the yogurt, cumin and honey in a bowl, then stir in the mint and season with salt and pepper, if using.

2. Add the beetroot, cucumber, radishes and spring onion, then gently toss together.

3. Arrange the lettuce leaves on a plate. Spoon a little of the salad into each leaf and serve immediately.

CUCUMBER &
BUCKWHEAT YOGURT

SERVES: 4 | **PREP:** *10 mins, plus soaking and chilling* | **COOK:** *No cooking*

INGREDIENTS

*1c ucumber, halved, deseeded and
   chopped*
*500 g/1 lb 2 oz plain dairy-free
   coconut yogurt*
3 tbsp chopped fresh mint
1 tsp sea salt
1 tsp pepper
100 g/3½ oz sun-dried raisins
70 g/2½ oz walnuts, chopped
125 g/4½ oz buckwheat groats
20 fresh mint leaves, to garnish

1. Soak the buckwheat groats in water for 20 minutes. Drain and rinse.

2. Wrap the cucumber pieces in kitchen paper and squeeze to release the moisture – the kitchen paper should be soaked.

3. Mix the yogurt, mint, salt and pepper together in a bowl.

4. Divide the ingredients between four 250–275-g/9–9¾-oz lidded jars. Layer with the raisins, half the walnuts, the soaked groats, three quarters of the cucumber and the yogurt mixture. Garnish with the remaining cucumber and walnuts.

5. Divide the mint leaves between the jars and chill in the refrigerator for 30 minutes before serving.

CHICKEN BALLS
WITH DIPPING SAUCE

SERVES: *4* | **PREP:** *25–30 mins* | **COOK:** *18–26 mins*

INGREDIENTS

2 large skinless, boneless chicken
*   breasts*
3 tbsp vegetable oil
2 shallots, finely chopped
½ celery stick, finely chopped
1 garlic clove, crushed
2 tbsp gluten-free tamari
1 small egg, lightly beaten
1 bunch of spring onions
salt and pepper (optional)

DIPPING SAUCE

3 tbsp gluten-free tamari
1 tbsp rice wine
1 tsp sesame seeds

1. Cut the chicken into 2-cm/¾-inch pieces. Heat half the oil in a frying pan, add the chicken and stir-fry over a high heat for 2–3 minutes until golden. Remove from the pan with a slotted spoon and set aside.

2. Add the shallots, celery and garlic and stir-fry for 1–2 minutes until soft.

3. Place the chicken and vegetables in a food processor and process until finely minced. Add 1 tablespoon of the tamari and enough of the egg to make a firm mixture. Season to taste with salt and pepper, if using.

4. To make the dipping sauce, mix together the tamari, rice wine and sesame seeds in a small serving bowl and set aside.

5. Shape the chicken mixture into 16 walnut-sized balls. Heat the remaining oil in the pan, add the balls in small batches and stir-fry for 4–5 minutes until golden. Drain on kitchen paper.

6. Add the spring onions to the pan and stir-fry for 1–2 minutes until they are beginning to soften, then stir in the remaining tamari. Serve the balls with the stir-fried spring onions and the dipping sauce.

SPICY FALAFELS

SERVES: *4* | **PREP:** *25 mins* | **COOK:** *10–15 mins*

INGREDIENTS

400 g/14 oz canned chickpeas,
drained and rinsed
1 small red onion, chopped
2 garlic cloves, crushed
2 tsp ground coriander
1½ tsp ground cumin
1 tsp ground star anise
1 fresh red chilli, chopped
1 egg white
½ tsp gluten-free baking powder
gram flour, for dusting
sunflower oil, for deep-frying
salt and pepper (optional)

SALAD

1 large orange
2 tbsp extra virgin olive oil
55 g/2 oz rocket leaves
salt and pepper (optional)

1. Place the chickpeas, onion, garlic, coriander, cumin, star anise, chilli, egg white, and salt and pepper, if using, in a blender or food processor and process to a firm, textured paste, then stir in the baking powder.

2. Dust your hands with a little flour and shape the mixture into 12 small balls.

3. To make the salad, cut all the peel and white pith from the orange and lift out the segments, catching the juice. Whisk the orange juice with the olive oil and season to taste with salt and pepper, if using. Lightly toss the orange segments and rocket with the dressing.

4. Heat a 2.5 cm/1 inch depth of oil in a large saucepan to 180–190°C/350–375°F, or until a cube of bread browns in 30 seconds. Add the falafels and fry for about 2 minutes until golden brown.

5. Drain the falafels on kitchen paper and serve with the salad.

CHAPTER THREE

LUNCH

CHILLED BEETROOT
& WATERMELON SOUP

SERVES: *4* | **PREP:** *10 mins, plus chilling* | **COOK:** *No cooking*

INGREDIENTS

4 tender beetroots, about 600 g/
  1 lb 5 oz
1 large carrot, about 175 g/6 oz
300 g/10½ oz watermelon flesh
juice of ½ lemon
1 tsp sea salt
1 tsp pepper
100 ml/3½ fl oz water
3 tbsp chopped fresh dill
150 g/5½ oz plain yogurt

1. Blend two thirds of the beetroots, carrot and watermelon in a blender with the lemon juice and most of the water until smooth. Add the salt and pepper, then add the water, a little at a time, and blend again to a medium-thick soup texture. Pour the soup into a large bowl.

2. Grate the remaining beetroot and carrot and stir into the soup. Chop the remaining watermelon into 1-cm/½-inch pieces and stir half of them into the soup with half the dill.

3. Pour the soup into four serving bowls and drizzle over the yogurt. Scatter the remaining watermelon pieces over the top and sprinkle over the remaining dill. Chill in the refrigerator before serving.

CHICKEN & VEGETABLE SOUP

SERVES: *4* | **PREP:** *15–20 mins* | **COOK:** *1 hour 20 mins*

INGREDIENTS

1 onion, finely chopped

1 garlic clove, finely chopped

115 g/4 oz white cabbage, shredded

2 carrots, finely chopped

4 potatoes, diced

1 green pepper, cored, deseeded and diced

400 g/14 oz canned chopped tomatoes

1.3 litres/2¼ pints gluten-free chicken stock

175 g/6 oz cooked chicken, diced

salt and pepper (optional)

2 tbsp chopped fresh flat-leaf parsley, to garnish

1. Put all the ingredients, except the chicken and parsley, in a large saucepan and bring to the boil. Simmer for 1 hour, or until the vegetables are tender.

2. Add the chicken and simmer for a further 10 minutes, or until heated through.

3. Ladle the soup into warmed bowls and serve immediately, garnished with the parsley.

SOUTH INDIAN
LENTIL BROTH

SERVES: *4* | **PREP:** *10 mins* | **COOK:** *30–35 mins*

INGREDIENTS

100 g/3½ oz pigeon peas (tuvaar dal)

600 ml/1 pint cold water

1 tsp ground turmeric

2 tbsp vegetable or groundnut oil

1 tsp black mustard seeds

6–8 fresh curry leaves

1 tsp cumin seeds

1 fresh green chilli, chopped

1 tsp tamarind paste

1 tsp salt

1. Rinse the pigeon peas under cold running water and place in a saucepan with the water, turmeric and 1 tablespoon of the oil. Cover, bring to a simmer and cook for 25–30 minutes, or until cooked and tender.

2. Heat the remaining oil in a frying pan over a medium heat. Add the mustard seeds, curry leaves, cumin seeds, chilli and tamarind paste. When the seeds start to pop, remove the pan from the heat and add to the pigeon pea mixture with the salt.

3. Return the broth to the heat for 2–3 minutes. Ladle into small bowls and serve immediately.

SPICY TOMATO, TAMARIND
& GINGER SOUP

SERVES: *4* | **PREP:** *15 mins* | **COOK:** *35 mins*

INGREDIENTS

60 g/2¼ oz butter

1 small onion, diced

2-cm/¾-inch piece fresh ginger,
  finely chopped

1 tsp ground turmeric

2 tsp cumin seeds, crushed

¼ tsp salt

½ tsp pepper

400 g/14 oz canned chopped
  tomatoes

2 tsp tamarind paste

70 g/2½ oz red quinoa, rinsed

225 ml/8 fl oz gluten-free vegetable
  stock

4 tbsp chopped fresh coriander

1. Heat half the butter in a large saucepan. Add the onion and fry over a low–medium heat for 5 minutes until translucent.

2. Add the ginger, turmeric, ½ teaspoon of the cumin seeds, the salt and pepper and cook for a further 1 minute.

3. Stir in the tomatoes, tamarind paste, quinoa and stock. Bring to the boil, then reduce the heat, cover and simmer for 25 minutes, stirring occasionally.

4. Remove from the heat and stir in the coriander. Leave to stand, covered, for 10 minutes.

5. Heat the remaining butter in a small frying pan over a medium-high heat. Add the remaining cumin seeds and sizzle for a few seconds. Swirl into the soup and serve immediately.

TURKEY WALDORF BOWL

SERVES: *4* | **PREP:** *20 mins* | **COOK:** *No cooking*

INGREDIENTS

3 tbsp gluten-free tahini
2 tbsp lime juice
2 tsp agave syrup
1 tsp gluten-free soy sauce
350 g/12 oz cooked turkey,
  shredded
2 celery sticks, thinly sliced
50 g/1¾ oz red cabbage, shredded
2 crisp apples, cored and chopped
100 g/3½ oz seedless red grapes,
  halved
100 g/3½ oz Chinese cabbage,
  shredded
75 g/2¾ ounces walnuts, toasted
50 g/1¾ oz pecan nuts, toasted
salt and pepper (optional)

1. Whisk together the tahini, lime juice, agave syrup and soy sauce and season to taste with salt and pepper, if using.

2. Lightly toss together the remaining ingredients, then toss again with the dressing.

3. Divide between four large shallow bowls and serve immediately.

ASIAN SALAD
WITH COCONUT RICE

SERVES: 6 | **PREP:** *20 mins, plus standing* | **COOK:** *25–30 mins*

INGREDIENTS

160 ml/5½ fl oz canned coconut
cream
450 ml/16 fl oz water
250 g/9 oz jasmine rice, rinsed
3 kaffir lime leaves
pinch of salt
½ large red cabbage, shredded
60 g/2¼ oz peanuts (unroasted),
roughly chopped
zest and juice of 1 lime
25 g/1 oz fresh coriander, roughly
chopped
25 g/1 oz fresh mint, roughly
chopped
1 spring onion, finely sliced
2 tbsp sesame oil
1 tbsp sesame seeds, toasted
pepper (optional)

1. Pour the coconut cream and water into a medium-sized pan and bring to the boil. Add the rice, lime leaves and salt. Reduce the heat, cover and cook over a low heat for 15–20 minutes until most of the liquid has been absorbed. Remove from the heat, cover and leave to stand for 5 minutes.

2. Stir the shredded cabbage through the rice along with half the peanuts, the lime zest and half the herbs. Season with pepper to taste, if using.

3. Spoon the rice mixture onto a serving plate and top with the spring onion, the remaining herbs and the peanuts. Spritz with lime juice and serve with a drizzle of sesame oil and a sprinkling of sesame seeds.

PANCETTA, SPINACH
& CHICKEN SALAD

SERVES: *4* | **PREP:** *30 mins* | **COOK:** *40 mins*

INGREDIENTS

5 skinless chicken thighs, about
* 450 g/1 lb total weight, halved*
1 tsp olive oil, for brushing
2–3 fresh thyme sprigs
300 g/10½ oz dried gluten-free
* pasta spirals*
150 g/5½ oz baby spinach, washed
100 g/3½ oz pancetta
½ red onion, very finely sliced
salt and pepper (optional)
2 tbsp snipped fresh chives, to
* garnish*

DRESSING

2 tbsp olive oil
1 garlic clove, crushed
1 tbsp gluten-free Dijon mustard
2 tbsp cider vinegar
salt and pepper (optional)

1. Preheat the oven to 200°C/400°F/Gas Mark 6.

2. Place the chicken thighs in a roasting tin and brush each with a little oil. Scatter over the thyme and season to taste with salt and pepper, if using.

3. Place in the centre of the oven and cook for 20 minutes until the chicken is tender and the juices run clear when a skewer is inserted into the thickest part of the meat. Remove from the oven and leave to cool.

4. Bring a large saucepan of water to the boil and add the pasta. Bring back to the boil and cook for 7–8 minutes until the pasta is tender but still firm to the bite. Drain, return to the pan and immediately stir the baby spinach through the pasta. The spinach will wilt in the residual heat.

5. Heat a medium-sized frying pan over a high heat, add the pancetta and fry until golden and crisp. Set aside.

6. Tear the cooled chicken into strips. Arrange the chicken, pancetta, pasta, spinach and red onion on a large platter.

7. To make the dressing, put the oil, garlic, mustard and vinegar in a jar. Add salt and pepper to taste, if using. Shake until the dressing is emulsified and smooth, then spoon it over the salad. Serve immediately, garnished with chives.

BUCKWHEAT
NOODLE SALAD

SERVES: *4* | **PREP:** *10 mins* | **COOK:** *10 mins*

INGREDIENTS

150 g/5½ oz gluten-free soba noodles

200 g/7 oz frozen edamame beans

225 g/8 oz broccoli, cut into small florets, stems thinly sliced

1 red pepper, halved, deseeded and thinly sliced

1 purple or orange pepper, halved, deseeded and thinly sliced

115 g/4 oz chestnut mushrooms, thinly sliced

85 g/3 oz ready-to-eat sprouting sunflower seeds

DRESSING

2 tbsp rice wine vinegar

2 tbsp gluten-free tamari

4 tbsp rice bran oil

4-cm/1½-inch piece fresh ginger, finely grated

1. Put some cold water in the base of a steamer, bring to the boil, then add the noodles and edamame beans and bring back to the boil. Put the broccoli in the top of the steamer, then place it on the steamer base, cover and steam for 3–5 minutes, or until the noodles and vegetables are just tender. Drain and rinse the noodles and edamame beans, then drain again and tip into a salad bowl. Add the broccoli, then leave to cool.

2. To make the dressing, put the vinegar, tamari, oil and ginger in a jam jar, screw on the lid and shake well. Drizzle over the salad and gently toss together.

3. Add the red and purple peppers and mushrooms to the salad and toss again. Spoon into four bowls, then top with the sprouting seeds and serve immediately.

RED QUINOA & CHICKPEA SALAD

SERVES: *4* | **PREP:** *10–15 mins* | **COOK:** *15–20 mins*

INGREDIENTS

50 g/1¾ red quinoa

1 red chilli, deseeded and finely chopped

8 spring onions, chopped

3 tbsp finely chopped fresh mint

2 tbsp olive oil

2 tbsp fresh lemon juice

30 g/1 oz chickpea (gram) flour

1 tsp ground cumin

½ tsp paprika

1 tbsp vegetable oil

150 g/5½ oz canned chickpeas, drained and rinsed

1. Place the quinoa in a medium-sized saucepan and cover with boiling water. Place over a low heat and simmer for 10 minutes, or until just cooked. Drain and refresh with cold water, then drain again. Transfer to a large bowl and toss with the red chilli, spring onion and mint.

2. Mix the olive oil and lemon juice together in a small bowl.

3. Sift together the chickpea flour, cumin and paprika into a wide, deep bowl. Place the vegetable oil in a medium frying pan over a medium heat. Roll the chickpeas in the spiced flour, then gently fry in the pan, stirring frequently, for 2–3 minutes, allowing the chickpeas to brown in patches.

4. Stir the warm chickpeas into the quinoa mixture and quickly stir in the lemon-oil dressing. Serve warm or chilled.

MELON, PARMA HAM & PECORINO SALAD

SERVES: *4* | **PREP:** *10–15 mins* | **COOK:** *No cooking*

INGREDIENTS

400 g/14 oz watermelon flesh, thinly sliced

400 g/14 oz honeydew melon flesh, thinly sliced

400 g/14 oz cantaloupe melon flesh, thinly sliced

140 g/5 oz sliced Parma ham

25 g/1 oz fresh pecorino cheese shavings

25 g/1 oz fresh basil

DRESSING

4 tbsp light olive oil

4 tbsp aged sherry vinegar

salt and pepper (optional)

1. Arrange the watermelon, honeydew melon and cantaloupe melon slices on a large serving platter. Tear any large Parma ham slices in half, then fold them all over and around the melon.

2. To make the dressing, put the oil and vinegar in a jam jar, season well with salt and pepper, if using, screw on the lid and shake well. Drizzle the dressing over the melon and Parma ham.

3. Sprinkle over the cheese and basil and serve immediately.

GINGERED CARROT & POMEGRANATE SALAD

SERVES: *4* | **PREP:** *10–15 mins, plus marinating* | **COOK:** *No cooking*

INGREDIENTS

350 g/12 oz carrots, finely grated

5-cm/2-inch piece fresh ginger, finely grated

1 small pomegranate, quartered

50 g/1¾ oz ready-to-eat sprouting seeds, such as alfalfa and radish sprouts

TOPPING

3 tbsp light olive oil

3 tsp red wine vinegar

3 tsp pomegranate molasses

salt and pepper (optional)

1. Put the carrots and ginger in a salad bowl. Flex the pomegranate pieces to pop out the seeds, prising any stubborn ones out with the tip of a small knife, and add to the bowl.

2. To make the dressing, put the oil, vinegar and pomegranate molasses in a jam jar, season with salt and pepper, if using, screw on the lid and shake well. Drizzle over the salad and gently toss together. Cover and marinate in the refrigerator for 30 minutes.

3. Sprinkle the sprouting seeds over the salad and serve.

CHICKPEA FRITTERS

SERVES: *4* | **PREP:** *20 mins* | **COOK:** *20 mins*

INGREDIENTS

125 g/4½ oz gluten-free self-raising
flour
1 egg, beaten
175 ml/6 fl oz milk
140 g/5 oz spring onions, thinly
sliced
400 g/14 oz canned chickpeas,
rinsed and drained
4 tbsp chopped fresh coriander
sunflower oil, for frying
salt and pepper (optional)
fresh coriander sprigs, to garnish

1. Sift the flour into a bowl and make a well in the centre. Add the egg and milk and stir into the flour, then whisk to a smooth batter.

2. Stir in the onions, chickpeas and coriander, then season well with salt and pepper, if using.

3. Heat the oil in a large, heavy-based frying pan and add tablespoons of the batter. Fry in batches for 4–5 minutes, turning once, until golden brown.

4. Serve the fritters stacked on warmed serving plates, garnished with coriander sprigs.

COURGETTE QUICHE

SERVES: *4* | **PREP:** *25–30 mins, plus chilling & cooling* | **COOK:** *55 mins–1 hour*

INGREDIENTS

200 g/7 oz gluten-free plain white
* flour blend, plus extra for dusting*
100 g/3½ oz butter
3 tbsp snipped fresh chives
pinch of salt
4–5 tbsp cold water
whole chives, to garnish

FILLING

2 tbsp olive oil
1 small red onion, cut into wedges
2 courgettes, cut into 2-cm/¾-inch
* chunks*
8 cherry tomatoes, halved
1 large egg, beaten
175 ml/6 fl oz milk
salt and pepper (optional)

1. Place the flour, butter, chives and salt in a food processor and process to fine crumbs. Add enough water to mix to a firm dough.

2. Turn out the dough onto a lightly floured work surface, roll out into a round and use to line a 19-cm/7½-inch diameter, 5-cm/2-inch deep, loose-based flan tin. Prick with a fork and chill in the refrigerator for 10 minutes.

3. Preheat the oven to 200°C/400°C/Gas Mark 6 and preheat a baking sheet. Line the pastry case with baking paper and baking beans and bake blind in the preheated oven for 10 minutes. Remove the paper and beans and bake for a further 5 minutes. Reduce the oven temperature to 190°C/375°F/Gas Mark 5.

4. To make the filling, heat the oil in a frying pan, add the onion and courgettes and fry, stirring frequently, for 4–5 minutes, or until soft and lightly browned. Tip into the pastry case with the tomatoes.

5. Beat the egg with the milk and season well with salt and pepper, if using. Pour into the pastry case. Bake in the preheated oven for 35–40 minutes, or until golden brown and set. Leave to cool in the tin for 10 minutes before turning out. Serve warm or cold, garnished with chives.

QUINOA PIZZA WITH CASHEW CHEESE

SERVES: 2 | **PREP:** 30 mins, plus soaking | **COOK:** 20 mins

INGREDIENTS

CASHEW CHEESE

60 g/2¼ oz cashew nuts, soaked in
    cold water overnight and drained
1 small garlic clove, crushed
1 tbsp nutritional yeast flakes
1½ teaspoons lemon juice

TOPPING

70 g/2½ oz drained sun-dried
    tomatoes in oil
3 tbsp gluten-free tomato purée
1 garlic clove, crushed
½ tsp salt (optional)
½ red pepper, deseeded and sliced
½ green pepper, deseeded and sliced
1 small red onion, cut into 6 wedges
2 tsp dried mixed herbs
2 tsp olive oil
5 artichoke hearts in oil, drained
1 tomato, roughly chopped

QUINOA BASE

125 g/4½ oz white quinoa, soaked
    in 475 ml/16 fl oz water for 8
    hours
½ tsp gluten-free baking powder
½ tsp salt
4 tbsp water
2 tbsp olive oil, plus extra for
    brushing

1. To make the cashew cheese, place the nuts in a food processor or blender with the garlic and 3 tablespoons of water. Process until smooth. Stir in the yeast and lemon juice and process for a few more seconds until it has a dropping consistency. Add a little extra water, if necessary, and blend again. Spoon into a bowl and set aside.

2. Preheat the oven to 190°C/375°F/Gas Mark 5. Line a 23-cm/9-inch shallow cake tin with baking paper and lightly oil the paper.

3. To make the quinoa base, drain the water from the quinoa and put into a blender with the baking powder, salt, water and 2 tablespoons of the oil. Blend to a thick, creamy batter. Transfer to the prepared tin and shape into a round. Bake in the preheated oven for 15 minutes, or until the top is golden. Remove from the tin, transfer to a wire rack and leave to cool.

4. Meanwhile, to make the topping, blend the sun-dried tomatoes with the tomato purée and garlic. Add salt, if using, and stir in a little water for a spreading consistency, if needed.

5. Toss the red and green peppers, onion and herbs with the olive oil and roast in a baking tray in the preheated oven for 10–15 minutes, or until soft and turning lightly golden. Remove from the heat and set aside.

6. Spread the tomato paste over the pizza base, leaving the edges clear. Arrange the peppers, onion, artichoke hearts and tomato on the pizza, then drop dollops of the cashew cheese over the top. Return to the oven for 5 minutes, or until the vegetables are hot and the cashew cheese is tinged golden and set.

SQUASH, PINE NUT & GOAT'S CHEESE PIZZA

SERVES: *6* | **PREP:** *30 mins* | **COOK:** *50–55 mins*

INGREDIENTS

1 egg white
3 tbsp vegetable oil
½ tsp vinegar
1 tbsp caster sugar
½ tsp salt
200 ml/7 fl oz water
250 g/9 oz gluten-free white bread
  flour
1 tsp gluten-free easy-blend dried
  yeast

PIZZA TOPPING

½ large squash, peeled, deseeded
  and cut into crescents
1 tbsp olive oil
3 fresh rosemary sprigs, roughly
  chopped
125 ml/4 fl oz soured cream
100 g/3½ oz goat's cheese, cut into
  rounds
50 g/1¾ oz pine nuts
pepper (optional)

1. Line a large oven tray with baking paper.

2. Put the egg white, half the vegetable oil, the vinegar, sugar, salt and water into a bowl and whisk well. Add the flour and yeast and mix until smooth and thick.

3. Pour the remaining oil over the batter and turn with a spoon until you have a soft dough. Spoon the dough onto the prepared tray and shape into a rough 25-cm/10-inch round. Leave to stand in a dry place for 30 minutes.

4. Meanwhile, preheat the oven to 200°C/400°F/Gas Mark 6. Place the squash crescents on a large baking tray and drizzle over the olive oil and half the rosemary.

5. Roast in the preheated oven for 20 minutes, turning the crescents halfway through, until they are beginning to turn golden. Remove from the oven and increase the oven temperature to 220°C/425°F/Gas Mark 7.

6. Spread the soured cream over the pizza base and top with the squash, goat's cheese, pine nuts and the remaining rosemary. Season to taste with pepper, if using.

7. Return to the oven and bake for 30–35 minutes until the base has puffed up and the cheese is golden and bubbling. Serve immediately.

PESTO SALMON WITH SPRING VEG BOWL

SERVES: *4* | **PREP:** *15 mins* | **COOK:** *10–12 mins*

INGREDIENTS

200 g/7 oz fresh or frozen peas
200 g/7 oz fresh broad beans
200 g/7 oz asparagus, woody stems
    discarded
200 g/7 oz baby carrots
4 skinless salmon fillets, each
    weighing 150 g/5½ oz
4 tbsp gluten-free basil pesto
4 tbsp extra virgin olive oil
grated rind and juice of 1 lemon
2 tbsp sunflower seeds, toasted
2 tbsp pumpkin seeds, toasted
2 tbsp shredded fresh basil

1. Place all the vegetables in a steamer and cook for 10–12 minutes, until tender.

2. Meanwhile, preheat the grill to hot and line a baking sheet with foil. Place the salmon on the prepared baking sheet and spoon over the pesto. Cook under the grill for 3–4 minutes on each side.

3. Mix the oil with the lemon rind and juice and toss with the cooked vegetables.

4. Divide the vegetables between four warmed shallow bowls and top each one with a salmon fillet.

5. Sprinkle with the sunflower seeds, pumpkin seeds and shredded basil and serve.

SWEET ROOTS BOWL

SERVES: *4* | **PREP:** *12 mins* | **COOK:** *35–40 mins*

INGREDIENTS

2 sweet potatoes, cut into chunks
2 beetroot, cut into chunks
2 red onions, cut into wedges
2 tbsp olive oil
2 tsp cumin seeds
75 g/2¾ oz brown rice
4 tbsp gluten-free tahini
juice of 1 lemon
½ tsp pepper
½ tsp clear honey
200 g/7 oz kale, shredded
2 tbsp flaked almonds, toasted

1. Preheat the oven to 200°C/400°F/Gas Mark 6.

2. Place the sweet potatoes, beetroot and onions in a bowl with the oil and cumin seeds and toss together to coat with the oil.

3. Tip into a roasting tin and roast in the preheated oven for 35–40 minutes until tender.

4. Meanwhile, cook the rice according to the packet instructions.

5. Whisk together the tahini, lemon juice, pepper and honey.

6. Stir the kale into the root vegetables 10 minutes before the end of the roasting time.

7. Drain the rice and divide between four warmed bowls.

8. Toss the vegetables with the dressing and serve on top of the rice, sprinkled with the toasted almonds.

SUSHI ROLL BOWL

SERVES: *4* | **PREP:** *15 mins, plus cooling* | **COOK:** *10 mins*

INGREDIENTS

300 g/10½ oz sushi rice

2 tbsp rice vinegar

1 tsp caster sugar

*1 large avocado, peeled, stoned and
    sliced*

200 g/7 oz raw tuna, sliced

200 g/7 oz raw salmon, sliced

juice of ½ lemon

4 sheets nori seaweed, shredded

¼ cucumber, cut into matchsticks

2 tbsp snipped fresh chives

1 tbsp black sesame seeds

4 tbsp gluten-free soy sauce, to serve

1. Cook the rice according to the packet instructions. When all the water has been absorbed and the rice is cooked, stir through the vinegar and sugar, then cover and leave to cool.

2. Divide the rice between four bowls.

3. Top each bowl with slices of avocado, tuna and salmon.

4. Squeeze over the lemon juice, then add the nori, cucumber, chives and sesame seeds.

5. Serve with the soy sauce.

TUNA & WASABI BURGERS WITH PICKLED VEGETABLES

SERVES: *4* | **PREP:** *40 mins, plus pickling* | **COOK:** *15 mins*

INGREDIENTS

4 tbsp rice wine vinegar

1 tbsp caster sugar

125 ml/4 fl oz water

½ tsp coriander seeds, crushed

½ tsp mustard seeds

½ cucumber, sliced

2 carrots, cut into ribbons

6 radishes, thinly sliced

3 shallots, thinly sliced

TUNA & WASABI BURGERS

400 g/14 oz tuna steaks, sliced into
*   2.5-cm/1-inch pieces*

25 g/1 oz fresh coriander, finely
*   chopped*

zest and juice of 1 lime

2 tsp gluten-free wasabi paste

4 spring onions, finely chopped

2 tbsp gluten-free mayonnaise

olive oil, for brushing

LIME CRÈME FRAÎCHE

4 tbsp crème fraîche

zest and juice of 1 lime

1. Heat the vinegar, sugar and water in a small saucepan over a medium heat until the sugar has dissolved. Remove from the heat and add the coriander seeds and mustard seeds.

2. Put the cucumber, carrots, radishes and shallots in a small bowl or sterilized jar and pour over the pickling liquid. Leave to pickle overnight, or for at least 4 hours.

3. Briefly pulse the tuna slices in a food processor until just chopped. Transfer to a large bowl and combine with the coriander, lime zest, lime juice, wasabi paste, spring onions and mayonnaise. Mix well and chill in the refrigerator for 15 minutes.

4. Meanwhile, make the lime crème fraîche. Combine the crème fraiche with the lime zest and juice in a bowl. Set aside.

5. Shape the tuna mixture into four burgers and brush each one with oil. Cook them in a griddle pan for 6 minutes on each side, or until they are cooked through.

6. Serve the burgers with the pickled vegetables and a dollop of lime crème fraîche.

BLACK BEAN & QUINOA BURRITOS

MAKES: 8 burritos | **PREP:** 30 mins | **COOK:** 20 mins

INGREDIENTS

60 g/2¼ oz red quinoa, rinsed

150 ml/5 fl oz water

2 tbsp vegetable oil

1 red onion, diced

1 fresh green chilli, deseeded and
    diced

1 small red pepper, deseeded and
    diced

400 g/14 oz canned black beans,
    drained and rinsed

juice of 1 lime

4 tbsp chopped fresh coriander

2 tomatoes

8 gluten-free corn tortillas, warmed

125 g/4½ oz Cheddar cheese,
    roughly grated

85 g/3 oz shredded cos lettuce

salt and pepper (optional)

1. Put the quinoa into a saucepan with the water. Bring to the boil, then cover and simmer over a very low heat for 15 minutes. Remove from the heat, but leave the pan covered for a further 5 minutes to allow the grains to swell. Fluff up with a fork and set aside.

2. Heat the oil in a frying pan. Fry half the onion, half the chilli and the red pepper until soft. Add the beans, quinoa, half the lime juice and half the coriander. Fry for a few minutes, then season to taste with salt and pepper, if using.

3. Halve the tomatoes and scoop out the seeds. Add the seeds to the bean mixture. Dice the tomato flesh and place in a bowl with the remaining coriander, onion, chilli and lime juice, and salt to taste, if using. Stir to combine.

4. Place 5 tablespoons of the bean mixture on top of each tortilla. Sprinkle with the tomato salsa, cheese and lettuce. Fold the end and sides over the filling, roll up and serve immediately.

CHAPTER FOUR

DINNER

COURGETTI WITH GARLIC CREAM SAUCE

SERVES: 2 | **PREP:** *20 mins, plus soaking* | **COOK:** *No cooking*

INGREDIENTS

2 courgettes, spiralized

1 tbsp cold-pressed extra virgin olive oil

½ tsp sea salt

GARLIC CREAM SAUCE

100 g/3½ oz skinned almonds, soaked in water for 2 hours, drained and rinsed

2 tbsp almond milk

1 large garlic clove, chopped

1 spring onion, chopped

2 tsp apple cider vinegar

½ tsp sea salt

TO SERVE

6 sun-dried tomato pieces

10 baby plum tomatoes, halved

1 spring onion, chopped

2 fresh basil sprigs

1. To make the garlic cream sauce, pulse the soaked almonds in a food processor until ground. Add the almond milk, garlic, spring onion, vinegar and salt and blend to a thick, creamy paste. Transfer to a bowl.

2. Toss the courgette spirals in the oil and salt and divide between two bowls.

3. Spoon the creamy sauce into the centre of each bowl, then top with the sun-dried tomatoes, plum tomatoes, spring onions and basil sprigs. Serve immediately.

QUINOA &
BEETROOT BURGERS

MAKES: *8 burgers* | **PREP:** *35 mins, plus chilling* | **COOK:** *1 hour 10 mins*

INGREDIENTS

3–4 small beetroots, peeled and
*   cubed, about 225 g/8 oz in total*
135 g/4¾ oz quinoa, rinsed
350 ml/12 fl oz gluten-free vegetable
*   stock*
½ small onion, grated
finely grated rind of ½ lemon
2 tsp cumin seeds
½ tsp salt
¼ tsp pepper
1 large egg white, lightly beaten
quinoa flour, for dusting
vegetable oil, for shallow-frying
8 slices gluten-free sourdough toast
*   and peppery green salad leaves,*
*   to serve*

WASABI BUTTER

1½ tsp gluten-free wasabi powder
¾ tsp warm water
70 g/2½ oz butter, at room
*   temperature*

1. Cook the beetroots in a steamer for 1 hour.

2. Meanwhile, put the quinoa into a saucepan with the stock. Bring to the boil, then cover and simmer over a very low heat for 10 minutes. Remove from the heat, but leave the pan covered for a further 10 minutes to allow the grains to swell. Fluff up with a fork and spread out on a tray to dry.

3. To make the wasabi butter, mix together the wasabi powder and water. Mix with the butter and chill in the refrigerator.

4. Place the beetroots in a food processor and process until smooth. Tip into a bowl and mix with the quinoa, onion, lemon rind, cumin seeds, salt, pepper and egg white.

5. Divide the mixture into eight equal-sized portions and shape the portions into 15-mm/⅝-inch thick burgers, firmly pressing the mixture together. Lightly dust with flour.

6. Heat a thin layer of oil in a non-stick frying pan. Add the burgers and fry over a medium–high heat, in batches if necessary, for 2 minutes on each side, turning carefully.

7. Place the burgers on the toast and serve with the wasabi butter and salad leaves.

MUSHROOM PASTA

SERVES: *4* | **PREP:** *15 mins* | **COOK:** *25–30 mins*

INGREDIENTS

300 g/10½ oz dried gluten-free
penne
2 tbsp olive oil
250 g/9 oz mushrooms, sliced
1 tsp dried oregano
250 ml/9 fl oz gluten-free vegetable
stock
1 tbsp lemon juice
6 tbsp plain cream cheese
200 g/7 oz frozen spinach leaves
salt and pepper (optional)

1. Add a little salt, if using, to a large saucepan of water and bring to the boil, then add the pasta and cook according to the packet instructions. Drain, reserving 175 ml/6 fl oz of the cooking liquid.

2. Meanwhile, heat the oil in a large, heavy-based frying pan over a medium heat, add the mushrooms and cook, stirring frequently, for 8 minutes until almost crisp. Stir in the oregano, stock and lemon juice and cook for 10–12 minutes, or until the liquid is reduced by half.

3. Stir in the cream cheese and spinach and cook over a medium–low heat for 3–5 minutes. Add the reserved cooking liquid, then the pasta. Stir well, season to taste with salt and pepper, if using, and heat through before serving.

JAMAICAN RICE & PEAS WITH TOFU

SERVES: *4* | **PREP:** *15 mins* | **COOK:** *15–20 mins*

INGREDIENTS

250 g/9 oz firm plain tofu, cubed
2 tbsp chopped fresh thyme, plus
*   extra sprigs to garnish*
2 tbsp olive oil
1 onion, sliced
1 garlic clove, crushed
1 small fresh red chilli, chopped
400 ml/14 fl oz gluten-free stock
200 g/7 oz basmati rice
4 tbsp coconut cream
400 g/14 oz canned red kidney
*   beans, drained and rinsed*
salt and pepper (optional)

1. Toss the tofu with half the chopped thyme and sprinkle with salt and pepper, to taste, if using.

2. Heat 1 tablespoon of the oil in a large pan, add the tofu and fry, stirring occasionally, for 2 minutes. Remove and keep warm.

3. Add the remaining oil to the pan, then add the onion and fry, stirring, for 3–4 minutes. Stir in the garlic, chilli and the remaining chopped thyme, then add the stock and bring to the boil. Stir in the rice, then reduce the heat, cover and simmer for 12–15 minutes until the rice is tender.

4. Stir in the coconut cream and beans, season to taste with salt and pepper, if using, and cook gently for 2–3 minutes. Spoon the tofu over the rice and serve hot, garnished with thyme sprigs.

CAULIFLOWER &
BUTTER BEAN STEW

SERVES: *4* | **PREP:** *20 mins* | **COOK:** *35 mins*

INGREDIENTS

2 tbsp olive oil

2 large red onions, sliced

2 carrots, cut into 2-cm/¾-inch dice

2 celery sticks, cut into 2-cm/
¾-inch dice

3 garlic cloves, crushed

400 g/14 oz canned plum tomatoes
in juice

250 ml/9 fl oz gluten-free vegetable
stock

1 tbsp gluten-free sun-dried tomato
purée

½ tbsp dried mixed herbs

½ tsp pepper

400 g/14 oz canned butter beans,
drained and rinsed

1 head of cauliflower, broken into
florets

salt (optional)

1 tsp sweet paprika, to garnish

1. Add the oil to a large lidded saucepan and place over a medium–high heat. Add the onions, carrots and celery and cook for 5 minutes, or until lightly coloured, stirring occasionally. Stir in the garlic and cook for 1 minute.

2. Add the canned tomatoes and their juices, roughly crushing any whole tomatoes against the side of the pan. Stir in the stock, tomato purée, mixed herbs, pepper, and salt, if using. Bring to a simmer, reduce the heat to low and cover. Cook for a further 20 minutes, or until all the vegetables are tender.

3. Stir in the butter beans and cook for a further 5 minutes. Place the cauliflower florets on top of the stew, replace the lid and simmer for a further 5 minutes, or until the cauliflower is just tender when the stalks are pierced with a sharp knife.

4. Serve the stew immediately, garnished with the sweet paprika.

SQUASH &
RED PEPPER PIE

SERVES: *8* | **PREP:** *55 mins* | **COOK:** *1 hour 55 mins–2 hours 15 mins*

INGREDIENTS

1 butternut squash, peeled and
  deseeded
3 large parsnips, scrubbed and
  trimmed
2 red peppers, deseeded
3 tbsp gluten-free harissa paste
1 tbsp olive oil
1 tsp salt
15 g/½ oz fresh coriander, chopped
100 ml/3½ fl oz water
1 kg/2 lb 4 oz floury potatoes,
  peeled
50 ml/2 fl oz milk
1 large garlic clove, crushed
salt and pepper (optional)

SPICED TOMATO SAUCE

2 tbsp olive oil
1 red onion, chopped
2 large garlic cloves, finely chopped
1 tsp cumin seeds
400 g/14 oz canned chopped plum
  tomatoes
1 tbsp soft light brown sugar
salt and pepper (optional)

1. Preheat the oven to 200°C/400°F/Gas Mark 6.

2. To make the spiced tomato sauce, heat the oil in a large, shallow casserole dish over a low heat. Add the onion and cook for 5 minutes. Stir through the garlic and cumin and cook for 2 minutes, stirring. Pour in the tomatoes, add the sugar and season to taste with salt and pepper, if using. Simmer for 30 minutes.

3. Meanwhile, chop the squash, parsnips and peppers into 3-cm/1¼-inch cubes and mix with the harissa paste, oil and salt in a large bowl. Scatter the vegetables in a large, shallow roasting tin. Roast in the preheated oven for 30 minutes, until the vegetables are beginning to caramelize.

4. Remove the roasted vegetables from the oven and mix into the tomato sauce with the coriander and water. Season to taste with salt and pepper, if using.

5. Halve the potatoes, place them in a large saucepan and cover with cold water. Bring to the boil and simmer for 20–25 minutes. Drain well. Return the potatoes to the pan, add the milk and garlic and mash until smooth.

6. Decant the roasted vegetable mixture into a 2-litre/3½-pint ovenproof dish and top with the mashed potato. Bake in the preheated oven for 30–40 minutes until golden. Serve immediately.

ROAST SALMON WITH SPICES, POMEGRANATE & CORIANDER

SERVES: *4* | **PREP:** *10 mins* | **COOK:** *15–20 mins*

INGREDIENTS

4 salmon fillets

2 tsp ras el hanout

1 tsp sea salt flakes

grated zest and juice of 1 unwaxed lemon

2 tsp olive oil

seeds from ½ pomegranate

4 tbsp roughly chopped fresh coriander

1. Preheat the oven to 180°C/350°F/Gas Mark 4. Cut out four rectangles of baking paper, each large enough to comfortably wrap a salmon fillet, and four slightly larger rectangles of foil. Lay each rectangle of baking paper over a rectangle of foil. Put a salmon fillet in the centre of each baking paper rectangle.

2. Sprinkle the fillets with the ras el hanout, salt, lemon zest and juice and oil, pomegranate seeds and coriander. Bring the long edges of the baking paper up together, then fold them down a few times to form a crisp pleat over the top of the salmon and tuck the short edges below. Repeat with the foil to make a secure parcel.

3. Put the parcels on a baking tray. Roast on a high shelf of the oven for 15–20 minutes, or until the fish is cooked through and flakes easily when pressed with a knife. Serve the parcels for people to unwrap at the table.

GRILLED MACKEREL WITH CAULIFLOWER COUSCOUS

SERVES: *4* | **PREP:** *15 mins* | **COOK:** *6 mins*

INGREDIENTS

CAULIFLOWER COUSCOUS

1 cauliflower, cut into small florets

1 tbsp extra virgin olive oil

juice and zest of 1 lime

*1 red chilli, deseeded and finely
    chopped*

4 spring onions, chopped

1 garlic clove, very finely chopped

*15 g/½ oz fresh flat-leaf parsley,
    chopped*

*10 g/¼ oz fresh mint leaves,
    chopped*

½ tsp sea salt

½ tsp pepper

MACKEREL

*4 skin-on mackerel fillets, about
    125 g/4½ oz each*

1 tbsp extra virgin olive oil

1 tsp smoked sweet paprika

1 lime, quartered

1. Grate the cauliflower until you have couscous-like 'grains'. Add the oil, lime juice and zest, chilli, spring onions, garlic, parsley, mint, salt and pepper. Mix thoroughly to combine.

2. Line a grill pan with foil and preheat the grill to high. Make three cuts across the skin sides of the fish with a sharp knife and rub in the oil and paprika. Grill skin side up for 5 minutes, or until crisp, then turn over with a spatula and cook for a further 1 minute.

3. Divide the cauliflower couscous between serving plates and top with the mackerel. Serve immediately with the lime wedges.

COCONUT FISH CURRY

SERVES: *4* | **PREP:** *20 mins* | **COOK:** *25–30 mins*

INGREDIENTS

3 tbsp sunflower oil
1 red pepper, sliced
1 tsp ground turmeric
½ tsp ground cumin
½ tsp ground coriander
½ tsp hot chilli powder
5 curry leaves
400 ml/14 fl oz coconut milk
150 ml/5 fl oz coconut cream
50 ml/2 fl oz water
400 g/14 oz canned chickpeas,
*   drained and rinsed*
100 g/3½ oz baby spinach
200 g/7 oz raw prawns, peeled and
*   deveined*
200 g/7 oz skinned cod fillet, cut
*   into chunks*
2 tsp mustard seeds
juice of 1 lime

CURRY PASTE

25 g/1 oz raw cashew nuts
3 shallots, chopped
1 large red chilli, chopped
25 g/1 oz fresh coriander
2 garlic cloves, chopped
2 tbsp grated fresh ginger

1. To make the curry paste, begin by toasting the cashew nuts. Heat a large frying pan over a medium heat. Add the nuts in a single layer. Cook, stirring frequently, until the nuts are light-golden brown. Put the shallots, red chilli, half the coriander, garlic, ginger and toasted cashew nuts into a small food processor and process to a smooth aromatic paste.

2. Heat the oil in a large, heavy-based saucepan over a medium heat. Add the red pepper and fry for 5 minutes, or until beginning to soften. Add the curry paste and fry gently for 3 minutes. Add the turmeric, cumin, coriander and chilli powder and fry for a further 1 minute.

3. Add the curry leaves, coconut milk, coconut cream and water. Increase the heat and bring to the boil, then reduce the heat and simmer for 10–15 minutes. Add the chickpeas and cook for a further 5 minutes, then add the spinach, prawns and cod and poach for 2–3 minutes.

4. Garnish with the mustard seeds, lime juice and remaining coriander and serve immediately.

BRIGHT GREEN MACKEREL
& BUTTER BEANS

SERVES: *4* | **PREP:** *20 mins* | **COOK:** *35–40 mins*

INGREDIENTS

2 tbsp olive oil

5 shallots, sliced

3 garlic cloves, sliced

150 g/5½ oz tenderstem broccoli

400 g/14 oz canned butter beans,
*   drained and rinsed*

2 courgettes, grated

100 ml/3½ fl oz gluten-free
*   vegetable stock*

100 ml/3½ fl oz double cream

10 g/¼ oz fresh basil, torn

4 x 90-g/3¼-oz mackerel fillets,
*   deboned but skin on*

salt and pepper (optional)

1. Preheat the oven to 180°C/350°F/Gas Mark 4.

2. Heat half the oil in a medium-sized deep frying pan over a high heat. Add the shallots and garlic and fry for 3–4 minutes until golden. Remove from the heat and set aside.

3. Bring a small saucepan of water to the boil and add the broccoli. Simmer for 5–6 minutes until it has just started to soften. Drain and set aside.

4. Transfer the shallots, garlic, butter beans, courgettes, stock, cream, half the basil and the broccoli to a 2-litre/3½-pint ovenproof dish and mix well. Cover with foil and transfer to the preheated oven for 20 minutes.

5. Heat the remaining oil in a large non-stick frying pan over a high heat. Place the mackerel fillets in the pan skin side down, gently applying pressure to the skin, and fry for 3 minutes until the skin is crispy. Remove from the pan without cooking the flesh side.

6. Remove the vegetables from the oven and take off the foil. Place the fillets on the bean mixture, skin side up. Season with salt and pepper to taste, if using, and return to the oven for 4–5 minutes until the mackerel is cooked. Serve garnished with the remaining basil.

CHICKEN PEPERONATA BOWL

SERVES: *4* | **PREP:** *15 mins* | **COOK:** *35 mins*

INGREDIENTS

2 red peppers, deseeded and sliced

2 yellow peppers, deseeded and sliced

1 tbsp olive oil

2 red onions, peeled and finely sliced

300 g/10½ oz gluten-free dried penne

4 skinless chicken breasts

2 garlic cloves, crushed

50 g/1¾ oz fresh basil, chopped

2 tbsp balsamic vinegar

2 tbsp fresh Parmesan cheese shavings

salt and pepper (optional)

1. To make the peperonata, place the red and yellow peppers and the oil in a frying pan over a medium heat. Cover and cook gently for 15 minutes. Add the onions and cook for a further 15 minutes.

2. Meanwhile, cook the penne according to the packet instructions.

3. Preheat a griddle pan to hot, add the chicken breasts and cook for 6–8 minutes on each side until cooked through.

4. Meanwhile, toss the garlic and basil into the pepper mixture, then add the vinegar and cook for 2–3 minutes.

5. Drain the penne and toss into the peperonata. Season to taste with salt and pepper, if using.

6. Slice the chicken breasts diagonally. Divide the penne between four warmed bowls. Top with the chicken and some Parmesan cheese shavings.

ITALIAN RICE WITH CHICKEN & CHERRY TOMATOES

SERVES: *6* | **PREP:** *20 mins* | **COOK:** *1 hour*

INGREDIENTS

250 g/9 oz brown rice, rinsed

6 boneless chicken thighs (about 550 g/1 lb 4 oz total weight)

2 tbsp olive oil

1 red onion, sliced

3 fresh thyme sprigs

juice and zest of 1 lemon

3 garlic cloves, bashed

200 g/7 oz cherry tomatoes

50 g/1¾ oz black olives, stoned and chopped

15 g/½ oz fresh basil, chopped

125 g/4½ oz buffalo mozzarella cheese, torn

40 g/1½ oz freshly grated Parmesan cheese

40 g/1½ oz pine nuts

salt and pepper (optional)

1. Preheat the oven to 180°C/350°F/Gas Mark 4.

2. Bring a large saucepan of water to the boil over a high heat. Reduce the heat, add the rice and cook for 25–30 minutes, or until tender but still firm to the bite.

3. Meanwhile, put the chicken thighs, 1 tablespoon of the oil, the onion, thyme, lemon juice and zest and garlic into a medium-sized roasting tin, season to taste with salt and pepper, if using, and roast in the preheated oven for 10 minutes.

4. Baste the chicken, add the tomatoes to the tin and cook for a further 10 minutes until the chicken is tender and the juices run clear when a skewer is inserted into the thickest part of the meat. Remove the from the oven and leave to cool.

5. Drain the rice and mix with the cooking juices, the onion, tomatoes, olives and basil.

6. Raise the oven temperature to 200°C/400°F/Gas Mark 6. Spoon the rice mixture into a medium-sized ovenproof dish and nestle the chicken thighs into the rice. Top with the mozzarella cheese and Parmesan cheese. Sprinkle over the pine nuts and drizzle with the remaining oil. Bake for a further 10 minutes, or until the mozzarella cheese is golden and bubbling.

CREOLE CHICKEN WITH CORIANDER PARSNIP RICE

SERVES: *4* | **PREP:** *15 mins* | **COOK:** *25 mins*

INGREDIENTS

2 tbsp extra virgin rapeseed oil

4 small chicken breast fillets, each sliced into 3 equal pieces

1 large onion, sliced

2 celery sticks, finely chopped

1 green pepper, deseeded and thinly sliced

1 yellow pepper, deseeded and thinly sliced

2 garlic cloves, crushed

1 tsp smoked paprika

300 g/10½ oz canned chopped tomatoes

1 tsp sea salt

1 tsp pepper

2 large parsnips, roughly chopped

1 tbsp raw hemp seeds

4 tbsp fresh coriander leaves

4 fresh coriander sprigs, to garnish

1. Heat half the oil in a large frying pan over a high heat. Add the chicken pieces and fry for 2 minutes, or until very lightly browned. Remove from the pan with a slotted spatula and transfer to a plate. Set aside.

2. Add the onion, celery and green and yellow peppers to the pan with half the remaining oil. Reduce the heat to medium and fry, stirring frequently, for about 10 minutes, or until the vegetables are soft and are just turning golden.

3. Stir in the garlic and paprika and cook for 30 seconds. Add the chopped tomatoes and half the salt and pepper. Return the chicken to the pan, bring to a simmer and cook for 10 minutes.

4. Meanwhile, put the parsnips into a food processor. Process on high until they resemble rice grains, then stir in the hemp seeds and the remaining salt and pepper.

5. Heat the remaining oil in a frying pan over a medium heat. Stir in the parsnip rice and stir-fry for 2 minutes, then stir through the coriander leaves. Serve the chicken mixture spooned over the parsnip rice and garnished with the coriander sprigs.

WHITE CHICKEN CHILLI

SERVES: *6* | **PREP:** *15 mins* | **COOK:** *40 mins*

INGREDIENTS

1 tbsp vegetable oil

1 onion, diced

2 garlic cloves, finely chopped

1 green pepper, deseeded and diced

1 small green jalapeño chilli,
deseeded and diced

2 tsp chilli powder

2 tsp dried oregano

1 tsp ground cumin

1 tsp salt

500 g/1 lb 2 oz canned cannellini
beans, drained and rinsed

700 ml/1¼ pints gluten-free chicken
stock

450 g/1 lb cooked chicken breasts,
shredded

juice of 1 lime

25 g/1 oz chopped fresh coriander,
plus extra leaves to garnish

1. Heat the oil in a large, heavy-based saucepan over a medium–high heat. Add the onion, garlic, green pepper and chilli and cook, stirring occasionally, for about 5 minutes, or until soft.

2. Add the chilli powder, oregano, cumin and salt to the pan and cook, stirring, for a further 30 seconds. Add the beans and stock and bring to the boil. Reduce the heat to medium–low and simmer gently, uncovered, for about 20 minutes.

3. Ladle about half of the bean mixture into a blender or food processor and purée. Return the purée to the pan along with the shredded chicken. Simmer for about 10 minutes, or until heated through. Stir in the lime juice and chopped coriander, garnish with coriander leaves and serve immediately.

TAMARIND TURKEY WITH COURGETTE NOODLES

INGREDIENTS

500 g/1 lb 2 oz turkey breast, diced

1½ tbsp gluten-free tamari

3 courgettes

1½ tbsp groundnut oil

85 g/3 oz small okra

2.5-cm/1-inch piece fresh galangal or ginger, grated

3 garlic cloves, crushed

1 large red chilli, finely chopped

1 lemon grass stalk, bashed

2 tbsp rice wine

TAMARIND SAUCE

1 tbsp tamarind paste

100 ml/3½ fl oz gluten-free chicken stock

2 tsp gluten-free Thai fish sauce

1 tbsp palm sugar

1 tsp cornflour

1. Toss the turkey pieces with 1 tablespoon of the tamari to coat and leave to marinate for 5 minutes.

2. Meanwhile, make the tamarind sauce by combining all the ingredients thoroughly in a small bowl. Slice the courgettes into thin ribbons, using a spiralizer, or vegetable peeler.

3. Add half the oil to a large frying pan set over a medium–high heat. Add the coated turkey pieces and stir-fry for 3 minutes, or until cooked through. Transfer the turkey to a warmed plate with a slotted spoon. Reduce the heat to medium.

4. Add the okra to the pan with the remaining oil and stir-fry for 2 minutes, stirring occasionally. Add the galangal, garlic, chilli, lemon grass, rice wine and the remaining tamari and stir for a further 2 minutes. Return the turkey pieces to the pan and add the tamarind sauce. Stir well to combine and simmer for 3 minutes. Add a little extra chicken stock or water if the sauce gets too thick.

5. While the sauce is simmering, steam the courgette noodles over a saucepan of boiling water for 30 seconds to soften and warm. Remove the lemon grass from the turkey mixture and serve immediately, with the noodles on the side.

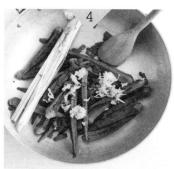

SAUSAGES WITH RED PEPPERS & GREEN LENTILS

SERVES: *4* | **PREP:** *20 mins* | **COOK:** *55 mins–1 hour 10 mins*

INGREDIENTS

250 g/9 oz green lentils, rinsed

5 tbsp olive oil

juice of ½ lemon

2 red peppers, deseeded and halved

6 large gluten-free pork sausages (about 400 g/14 oz)

1 garlic bulb, halved

3 fresh rosemary sprigs

salt and pepper (optional)

1. Preheat the oven to 200°C/400°F/Gas Mark 6.

2. Place the lentils in a large saucepan over a high heat and cover with water. Bring to the boil, then reduce the heat to a simmer and cook for 15–20 minutes, or until the lentils are tender but still firm to the bite. Strain. Stir though 2 tablespoons of the oil and the lemon juice. Season to taste with salt and pepper, if using.

3. Preheat the grill to hot. Place the red pepper halves on a baking tray, cut side down, and grill for 15–20 minutes, or until they are charred and completely blackened. Place in a bowl, cover with clingfilm and leave to cool, then peel off the charred skin and slice into strips.

4. Mix the peppers with the lentils and spread on a baking tray. Add the sausages, garlic and rosemary, drizzle over the remaining oil and bake in the preheated oven for 25–30 minutes, or until the sausages are brown and cooked through. Serve immediately.

CHIMICHURRI
STEAK

INGREDIENTS

675–900 g/1 lb 8 oz–2 lb sirloin
  steak
4 fresh corn cobs
1 shallot
3 garlic cloves
4 tbsp sherry vinegar or red wine
  vinegar
60 g/2¼ oz fresh flat-leaf parsley
1 tbsp fresh oregano leaves
½ tsp crushed red pepper flakes
125 ml/4 fl oz olive oil
juice of 1 lemon
salt and pepper (optional)

1. Preheat the grill to medium–high. Generously season the steak with salt and pepper, if using. Remove the corn husks and silks and wrap the cobs individually in foil.

2. Finely chop the shallot and garlic and place in a small bowl with the vinegar and 1 teaspoon of salt, if using. Finely chop the parsley and oregano and add them to the vinegar mixture along with the red pepper flakes. Whisk in the oil until well combined. Stir in the lemon juice. Put the corn and the steak on the grill rack. Cook the steak, turning once, for about 4 minutes on each side for medium-rare, or until nicely seared on the outside. Turn the corn occasionally, cooking it for 15 minutes in total.

3. Transfer the meat to a chopping board and leave to rest for 4 minutes. Slice it against the grain into 5-mm/¼-inch thick slices. Serve drizzled with the sauce and with the corn on the side.

STEAK & CHIPS WITH
WATERCRESS BUTTER

SERVES: *4* | **PREP:** *25 mins, plus chilling* | **COOK:** *45 mins–1 hour*

INGREDIENTS

85 g/3 oz unsalted butter, softened

4 tbsp finely chopped watercress,
*   plus extra sprigs to garnish*

4 sirloin steaks, about 225 g/8 oz
*   each*

4 tsp gluten-free hot pepper sauce

salt and pepper (optional)

CHIPS

450 g/1 lb potatoes, peeled

2 tbsp sunflower oil

1. To make the chips, preheat the oven to 200°C/400°F/Gas Mark 6. Cut the potatoes into thick, even-sized chips. Rinse them under cold running water, then dry well on a clean tea towel. Place in a bowl, add the oil and toss together until coated.

2. Spread the chips in a single layer on a baking sheet and cook in the preheated oven for 40–45 minutes, turning once, or until golden.

3. Place the butter in a small bowl and beat in the watercress with a fork until fully incorporated. Cover with clingfilm and leave to chill until required.

4. Preheat a griddle pan to high. Sprinkle each steak with 1 teaspoon of the hot pepper sauce, rubbing it in well. Season to taste with salt and pepper, if using.

5. Cook the steaks in the preheated pan for 2½ minutes on each side for rare, 4 minutes on each side for medium and 6 minutes on each side for well done. Transfer to warmed serving plates and serve immediately, topped with the watercress butter, garnished with watercress and accompanied by the chips.

SWEET & SPICY
MEATBALLS

SERVES: *4* | **PREP:** *20 mins, plus chilling* | **COOK:** *45–50 mins*

INGREDIENTS
MEATBALLS

400 g/14 oz fresh beef mince

5½ tsp chilli flakes

*50 g/1¾ oz dried apricots, finely
    chopped*

2 spring onions, finely chopped

1 egg

2 tbsp gluten-free plain flour

1 tbsp olive oil

salt and pepper (optional)

*1 tbsp chopped fresh flat-leaf
    parsley, to garnish*

steamed white rice, to serve

TOMATO SAUCE

1 tbsp olive oil

½ onion, roughly chopped

3 garlic cloves, sliced

1 tsp ground cumin

1 tbsp gluten-free tomato purée

*400 g/14 oz canned chopped
    tomatoes*

salt and pepper (optional)

1. To make the tomato sauce, heat the oil in a saucepan over a
medium heat. Add the onion and cook for 4–5 minutes. Remove the
pan from the heat and leave to cool.

2. Meanwhile, to make the meatballs, put the mince, chilli flakes,
apricots and spring onions in a large bowl. Lightly beat the egg and
add to the mixture. Add salt and pepper, if using, and combine.

3. Divide the mixture into 12 equal-sized balls. Sprinkle the flour onto
a plate and roll the meatballs in the flour. Chill in the refrigerator for
10 minutes.

4. Heat the oil in a frying pan, add the meatballs and cook for 5
minutes over a medium–high heat without moving them. Turn and
cook for a further 5 minutes, then remove from the pan and set aside
until needed.

5. Transfer the cooled onion to the frying pan with the garlic and
cumin. Cook over a medium–low heat for 1–2 minutes, then add the
tomato purée and tomatoes. Season with salt and pepper, if using.

6. Cook the sauce for 2–3 minutes, then add the meatballs to the
pan. Cover and gently cook for 20 minutes, or until the meatballs are
cooked through. Garnish with chopped parsley and serve with rice.

BEEF & BRASSICA
STIR-FRY

SERVES: *4* | **PREP:** *8 mins* | **COOK:** *8–12 mins*

INGREDIENTS

zest and juice of 1 orange
2 tbsp gluten-free soy sauce
2 tbsp sesame oil
250 g/9 oz purple sprouting
  broccoli, trimmed
200 g/7 oz cauliflower, broken into
  florets
1 tbsp coconut oil
5-cm/2-inch piece fresh ginger,
  peeled and shredded
1 garlic clove, peeled and sliced
1 red chilli, deseeded and diced
400 g/14 oz sirloin steak, cut into
  thin strips
1 red pepper, deseeded and thinly
  sliced
55 g/2 oz mangetout, shredded
2 tbsp sesame seeds, toasted

1. Mix the orange zest and juice, soy sauce and sesame oil together in a bowl.

2. Bring a large saucepan of water to the boil, add the broccoli and cauliflower and blanch for 2 minutes, then drain.

3. Heat the coconut oil in a wok or large frying pan and add the ginger, garlic, chilli and steak and stir-fry until the steak is brown all over. Remove with a slotted spoon.

4. Add the red pepper, mangetout, broccoli and cauliflower, pour in the orange juice mixture, cover and cook for 2–3 minutes.

5. Return the steak to the wok, stir-fry for 1–2 minutes, then serve in warmed bowls, sprinkled with the toasted sesame seeds.

LAMB KOFTAS

SERVES: 4 | **PREP:** 25 mins plus chilling | **COOK:** 30 mins

INGREDIENTS

250 g/9 oz fresh lean lamb mince
1 onion, finely chopped
1 tbsp chopped fresh coriander
1 tbsp chopped fresh parsley
½ tsp ground coriander
¼ tsp chilli powder
vegetable oil, for brushing
salt and pepper (optional)

CHICKPEA MASH

1 tbsp olive oil
2 garlic cloves, chopped
400 g/14 oz canned chickpeas,
    drained and rinsed
50 ml/2 fl oz milk
2 tbsp chopped fresh coriander
salt and pepper (optional)
fresh coriander sprigs, to garnish

1. You will need wooden skewers for this recipe. Put the lamb, onion, herbs, spices, and salt and pepper to taste, if using, in a food processor and process until thoroughly combined.

2. Divide the mixture into 12 portions and, using wet hands, shape each portion into a sausage shape around a wooden skewer (soaked in water first to prevent burning). Cover and chill the skewers in the refrigerator for 30 minutes.

3. To cook, preheat a griddle pan over a medium heat and brush with a little oil. Cook the skewers in two batches, turning occasionally, for 10 minutes, or until brown all over and cooked through.

4. To make the chickpea mash, heat the oil in a saucepan, add the garlic and gently fry for 2 minutes. Add the chickpeas and milk and heat through for a few minutes. Transfer to a food processor or blender and process until smooth. Season to taste with salt and pepper, if using, then stir in the fresh coriander. Garnish with coriander sprigs and serve with the koftas.

CHAPTER FIVE

DESSERTS
& BAKING

RHUBARB &
BLACKBERRY CRUMBLE

SERVES: *6* | **PREP:** *25 mins* | **COOK:** *50–55 mins*

INGREDIENTS

8–10 sticks rhubarb, about 800 g/
1 lb 12 oz, cut into bite-sized
pieces
8 tbsp caster sugar
250 g/9 oz blackberries
½ tsp vanilla extract
½ tsp ground ginger

CRUMBLE TOPPING

100 g/3½ oz butter, plus extra for
greasing
200 g/7 oz gluten-free plain flour
100 g/3½ oz demerara sugar
15 g/½ oz flaked almonds

1. Preheat the oven to 180°C/350°F/Gas Mark 4. Grease a 23-cm/9-inch ovenproof dish.

2. Place the rhubarb on a baking tray, sprinkle with the caster sugar and bake in the preheated oven for 12–15 minutes.

3. Transfer the rhubarb to the prepared dish and add the blackberries, vanilla extract and ginger.

4. To make the topping, rub the butter and flour together with your fingertips until the mixture resembles fine breadcrumbs. Add the demerara sugar and almonds. Cover the rhubarb with the crumble topping and bake for 35–40 minutes until golden.

CREAMY COCONUT & MANGO QUINOA

SERVES: *4* | **PREP:** *15 mins, plus standing* | **COOK:** *25–30 mins*

INGREDIENTS

300 ml/10 fl oz canned coconut
milk
115 g/4 oz white quinoa, rinsed
1 large ripe mango, about 550 g/
1 lb 4 oz
75 g/2¾ oz caster sugar
juice of 1 large lime
4-cm/1½-inch piece fresh ginger,
cut into chunks
100 g/3½ oz blueberries
4 tbsp toasted coconut chips
4 lime wedges, to decorate

1. Put the coconut milk and quinoa into a small saucepan over a medium heat and bring to the boil. Reduce the heat, cover and simmer for 15–20 minutes, or until most of the liquid has evaporated. Remove from the heat, but leave the pan covered for a further 10 minutes to allow the grains to swell. Fluff up with a fork, tip into a bowl and leave to cool.

2. Meanwhile, peel the mango, discard the stone and roughly chop the flesh (you will need 350 g/12 oz). Put the mango into a food processor with the sugar and lime juice. Squeeze the ginger in a garlic press and add the juice to the mango mixture. Process for 30 seconds to a smooth purée.

3. Mix the mango mixture into the cooled quinoa and leave to stand for 30 minutes.

4. Divide the mixture between four bowls and sprinkle with the blueberries and coconut chips. Decorate with lime wedges and serve.

PUMPKIN PIE SMOOTHIE BOWL

SERVES: *4* | **PREP:** *15 mins* | **COOK:** *12–15 mins*

INGREDIENTS

800 g/1 lb 12 oz pumpkin or
butternut squash, peeled,
deseeded and chopped

2 bananas, chopped

1 tbsp coconut oil

½ tsp ground cinnamon

3 tbsp maple syrup

400 g/14 oz plain Greek strained
yogurt

3 tbsp pumpkin seeds, toasted

2 tbsp sesame seeds, toasted

¼ tsp freshly grated nutmeg

1. Place the pumpkin in a saucepan with some water, bring to the boil, then simmer for 12–15 minutes until tender.

2. Drain, return to the pan and add the bananas, coconut oil, cinnamon and maple syrup. Mash to a smooth consistency.

3. Divide between four bowls and top each serving with some yogurt.

4. Sprinkle over the pumpkin seeds, sesame seeds and nutmeg and serve hot or cold.

COCONUT RICE PUDDING
WITH POMEGRANATE

SERVES: *4* | **PREP:** *15 mins, plus chilling* | **COOK:** *45–50 mins*

INGREDIENTS

55 g/2 oz pudding rice

*200 ml/7 fl oz canned light coconut
milk*

200 ml/7 fl oz almond milk

25 g/1 oz golden caster sugar

1 cinnamon stick

2 sheets leaf gelatine

*1 pomegranate, separated into
seeds*

*¼ tsp freshly grated nutmeg, for
sprinkling*

1. Place the rice, coconut milk, almond milk, sugar and cinnamon in a saucepan over a high heat. Bring almost to the boil, stirring, then reduce the heat, cover and simmer very gently, stirring occasionally, for 40–45 minutes, or until most of the liquid is absorbed

2. Meanwhile, place the gelatine in a bowl and cover with cold water. Leave to soak for 10 minutes to soften. Drain, squeezing out any excess moisture, then add the gelatin to the hot rice mixture and lightly stir until completely dissolved.

3. Spoon the rice mixture into four 150-ml/5-fl oz metal pudding basins, spreading evenly. Leave to cool, then cover and chill in the refrigerator until firm.

4. Run a small knife around the edge of each basin. Dip the bases briefly into a bowl of hot water, then turn out the rice onto four serving plates.

5. Scatter the pomegranate seeds over the rice, then sprinkle with grated nutmeg. Serve immediately.

MANGO CHEESECAKE

SERVES: *8* | **PREP:** *20 mins, plus cooling & chilling* | **COOK:** *40–45 mins*

INGREDIENTS

70 g/2½ oz butter, plus extra for greasing

175 g/6 oz gluten-free biscuits, such as digestives, crushed

40 g/1½ oz ground almonds

FILLING

1 large mango, stoned, peeled and diced

juice of 1 lemon

200 g/7 oz natural yogurt

1 tbsp gluten-free cornflour

3 tbsp maple syrup

450 g/1 lb plain cream cheese

TOPPING

3 tbsp maple syrup

1 small mango, stoned, peeled and sliced

1. Preheat the oven to 180°C/350°F/Gas Mark 4. Lightly grease a 23-cm/9-inch round, loose-based cake tin. To make the biscuit base, melt the butter in a medium-sized saucepan, then stir in the crushed biscuits and almonds. Press the mixture evenly into the base of the prepared tin. Bake in the preheated oven for 10 minutes.

2. Meanwhile, to make the filling, put the mango, lemon juice, yogurt, cornflour, maple syrup and cream cheese into a food processor or blender and process until smooth and creamy. Pour the mixture over the biscuit base and smooth with the back of a spoon. Bake for 25–30 minutes, or until golden and set. Leave to cool in the tin, then transfer to a wire rack and chill in the refrigerator for 30 minutes to firm up.

3. To make the topping, heat the maple syrup in a saucepan. Brush the top of the cheesecake with the maple syrup. Add the mango to the remaining maple syrup in the pan and cook for 1 minute, stirring. Leave to cool slightly, then arrange the mango slices on top of the cheesecake. Pour over any remaining syrup before serving.

PEACH &
ORANGE GRANITA

SERVES: *4* | **PREP:** *10 mins, plus freezing* | **COOK:** *No cooking*

INGREDIENTS

juice of 2 large oranges
4 peaches, stoned and peeled
juice of 1 lime
3 tbsp raw agave nectar
seeds from ½ vanilla pod
1 orange, cut into slices, to decorate
4 fresh mint leaves, to decorate

1. Put the orange juice, peaches, lime juice, agave nectar and vanilla seeds in a blender and blend until smooth, or until a few small peach pieces are left.

2. Pour the mixture into a shallow, lidded, freezer-proof container and freeze for 2 hours.

3. Stir the mixture with a fork, bringing the frozen edges into the centre. Replace the lid and freeze for a further 2 hours.

4. Stir again and freeze for a further 1 hour, or until nearly frozen in the centre. Stir again before dividing the granita between four glasses. Serve decorated with the orange slices and mint leaves.

PECAN PIE

SERVES: *12* | **PREP:** *40 mins, plus chilling* | **COOK:** *50–55 mins*

INGREDIENTS

PASTRY

200 g/7 oz gluten-free plain flour,
*   sifted, plus extra for dusting*
25 g/1 oz rice flour
2 tbsp gluten-free icing sugar
½ tsp xanthan gum
¼ tsp salt
115 g/4 oz butter, plus extra for
*   greasing*
1 egg, beaten
2 tbsp cold water

FILLING

115 g/4 oz caster sugar
3 large eggs
5 tbsp golden syrup
2 tbsp Bourbon
50 g/1¾ oz butter, melted
½ tsp vanilla extract
175 g/6 oz pecan halves
vanilla ice cream, to serve

1. Preheat the oven to 180°C/350°F/Gas Mark 4. Grease a 4-cm/1½-inch deep, 23-cm/9-inch fluted loose-based flan tin.

2. Place the plain flour, rice flour, icing sugar, xanthan gum and salt in a mixing bowl. Add the butter and rub it in until it resembles fine breadcrumbs.

3. Make a well in the centre of the mixture and add the egg and a little water. Using your hands, mix in the dry ingredients until a dough forms. Turn out onto a floured work surface and knead well. Wrap in clingfilm and chill in the refrigerator for 20–30 minutes.

4. Roll out the pastry to a thickness of 3 mm/⅛ inch and use it to line the prepared tin. Line with baking paper and baking beans and bake blind in the preheated oven for 12 minutes until golden. Remove the baking paper and beans.

5. To make the filling, whisk the sugar and the eggs in a bowl. Slowly stir in the golden syrup, Bourbon, butter and vanilla extract. Scatter the nuts over the pastry case. Pour the filling over the nuts and return to the oven. Bake for 35–40 minutes until just golden, then remove from the oven. Serve warm or cold with vanilla ice cream.

BLACK RICE PUDDING
WITH RASPBERRY COULIS

SERVES: *2* | **PREP:** *15 mins, plus cooling* | **COOK:** *50 mins*

INGREDIENTS

150 g/5½ oz black rice

1 large ripe banana, chopped

100 ml/3½ fl oz almond milk

2 tbsp agave syrup

1 tsp vanilla extract

150 g/5½ oz raspberries

1 tbsp fresh lemon juice

125 g/4½ oz natural yogurt

1 tbsp dried rose petals

25 g/1 oz pumpkin seeds

1. Place the rice in a medium-sized saucepan over a high heat, cover with water and bring to the boil. Reduce the heat and simmer for 40–45 minutes until just tender. Drain and leave to cool.

2. Whizz the banana, almond milk, 1 tablespoon of the agave syrup and the vanilla extract in a blender together with half the cooked rice. Stir through the remaining rice and set aside.

3. Blend the raspberries, the remaining agave syrup and lemon juice until smooth.

4. Spoon the sweetened rice into the base of two glasses. Add a layer of the raspberry coulis and spoon over the yogurt. Serve sprinkled with the rose petals and pumpkin seeds.

COCONUT MILK &
STRAWBERRY ICE CREAM

SERVES: 6 | **PREP:** *30 mins, plus freezing* | **COOK:** *No cooking*

INGREDIENTS

450 g/1 lb strawberries, hulled and
*   halved*
400 ml/14 fl oz canned full-fat
*   coconut milk*
85 g/3 oz clear honey
chopped hazelnuts, to serve

1. Purée the strawberries in a food processor or liquidizer, then press through a sieve set over a mixing bowl to remove the seeds.

2. Add the coconut milk and honey to the strawberry purée and whisk together.

3. Pour the mixture into a large roasting tin to a depth of 2 cm/¾ inch, cover the top of the tin with clingfilm, then freeze for about 2 hours until just set.

4. Scoop back into the food processor or liquidizer and blitz again to break down the ice crystals. Pour into a plastic container or 900-g/ 2-lb loaf tin lined with non-stick baking paper. Cover and return to the freezer for 3–4 hours, or until firm enough to scoop.

5. Serve immediately or leave in the freezer overnight or until needed. Thaw at room temperature for 15 minutes to soften slightly, then scoop into individual dishes and serve with a sprinkling of chopped hazelnuts.

FRUIT BREAD WITH
MACADAMIA NUTS

MAKES: *1 loaf* | **PREP:** *10 mins, plus soaking* | **COOK:** *1 hour–1 hour 30 mins*

INGREDIENTS

200 g/7 oz mixed dried fruit
350 ml/12 fl oz black tea
butter, for greasing and to serve
100 g/3½ oz figs
100 g/3½ oz macadamia nuts
zest of 1 orange
2 eggs, beaten
275 g/9¾ oz gluten-free self-raising
  flour
200 g/7 oz soft dark brown sugar

1. Place the dried fruit in a bowl and pour over the tea. Cover and leave the fruit to soak overnight.

2. The next day, preheat the oven to 180°C/350°F/Gas Mark 4. Grease a 900-g/2-lb loaf tin and line with baking paper.

3. Add the figs, macadamia nuts, orange zest, eggs, flour and sugar to the fruit mixture and combine well.

4. Pour the mixture into the prepared tin and smooth the surface. Bake in the preheated oven for 1–1½ hours until a skewer inserted into the middle of the cake comes out clean.

5. Turn out of the tin and transfer to a wire rack to cool, then slice and serve with butter.

CHOCOLATE, CHERRY & ALMOND FUDGE BITES

MAKES: *approx. 35 squares* | **PREP:** *10 mins, plus chilling* | **COOK:** *No cooking*

INGREDIENTS

*100 g/3½ oz unsweetened almond
    butter*

5 tbsp coconut oil

65 g/2¼ oz raw cacao powder

6 tbsp clear honey

¼ tsp sea salt

seeds from ½ vanilla pod

60 g/2¼ oz dried cherries

1. Blend the almond butter and coconut oil in a food processor for a few seconds to combine. Add the cacao powder and blend again.

2. Stir in the honey, salt and vanilla seeds and blend again. Stir in the dried cherries but do not blend.

3. Line a shallow 13 x 10-cm/5 x 4-inch tin or tray with baking paper, leaving the paper to overhang the edges by at least 5 cm/2 inches. Spoon the mixture into the prepared tin and level the surface. Chill in the freezer for about 1 hour, or until firm.

4. Remove the fudge from the tin using the overhanging paper. Place on a chopping board and, using a sharp knife, cut into five slices lengthways. Then cut each slice into seven squares. Serve or store in an airtight container in the refrigerator.

ROASTED HAZELNUT SHORTBREAD

MAKES: *18 pieces* | **PREP:** *20 mins* | **COOK:** *10–15 mins*

INGREDIENTS

90 g/3¼ oz gluten-free icing sugar

190 g/6½ oz gluten-free plain flour, plus extra for dusting

60 g/2¼ oz gluten-free cornflour

35 g/1¼ oz chopped roasted hazelnuts

25 g/1 oz ground almonds

250 g/9 oz butter, plus extra for greasing

½ tsp vanilla extract

caster sugar, for dusting

1. Preheat the oven to 180°C/350°F/Gas Mark 4. Grease one or two baking trays and line them with baking paper.

2. Put the dry ingredients into a bowl and rub in the butter and vanilla extract until a dough forms.

3. Turn out the dough onto a floured work surface and lightly knead. Roll out to a thickness of 1 cm/½ inch. Cut out 16–18 rounds using a 7-cm/2¾-inch cutter and place on the baking tray.

4. Bake in the preheated oven for 10–15 minutes until golden. Remove from the oven and dust with caster sugar while still warm. Transfer to a wire rack and leave to cool.

RASPBERRY & CHOCOLATE CAKE

SERVES: *12* | **PREP:** *20–25 mins* | **COOK:** *45–50 mins*

INGREDIENTS

margarine, for greasing
300 g/10½ oz gluten-free plain flour
50 g/1¾ oz pure dark cocoa powder
1 tsp gluten-free baking powder
1 tsp gluten-free bicarbonate of
soda
½ tsp salt
300 g/10½ oz granulated sugar
375 ml/13 fl oz milk
125 ml/4 fl oz rapeseed oil
7 tbsp seedless raspberry jam
1 tsp vanilla extract

ICING

40 ml/1½ fl oz milk
85 g/3 oz gluten-free plain
chocolate, broken into small
pieces
60 g/2¼ oz gluten-free icing sugar
1 tbsp maple syrup

1. Preheat the oven to 180°C/350°F/Gas Mark 4. Grease a 23-cm/9-inch cake tin and line with baking paper.

2. Sift together the flour, cocoa powder, baking powder and bicarbonate of soda into a large mixing bowl and stir in the salt and sugar. Pour the milk into a medium-sized saucepan and add the oil, raspberry jam and vanilla extract. Place over a medium heat and whisk to combine. Stir into the dry ingredients and mix thoroughly.

3. Transfer the mixture to the prepared tin and bake in the preheated oven for 45 minutes, or until a skewer inserted into the centre comes out clean. Transfer to a wire rack and leave to cool completely.

4. To make the icing, heat the milk in a small saucepan over a medium heat until it reaches boiling point, then drop the chocolate into the pan and stir until completely melted. Remove from the heat and whisk in the icing sugar and maple syrup. Leave to cool, then use to ice the cake with a palette knife.

BUTTER BEAN, HONEY & ORANGE CAKE

SERVES: *8* | **PREP:** *25 mins* | **COOK:** *45 mins*

INGREDIENTS

butter, for greasing

400 g/14 oz canned butter beans, drained and rinsed

175 g/6 oz caster sugar

3 eggs

150 g/5½ oz gluten-free self-raising flour

1 tsp clear honey

zest of 2 oranges

25 g/1 oz desiccated coconut

1 tsp gluten-free baking powder

COCONUT & ORANGE ICING

400 ml/14 fl oz canned coconut milk, chilled overnight

55 g/2 oz gluten-free icing sugar, sifted

zest of 1 orange

25 g/1 oz flaked almonds, toasted

1. Preheat the oven to 180°C/350°F/Gas Mark 4. Grease an 18-cm/7-inch cake tin and line it with baking paper.

2. Pulse the butter beans with the caster sugar in a food processor, then add the eggs one at a time. Continue to pulse while adding the flour and honey. Add the orange zest, coconut and baking powder.

3. Pour the mixture into the prepared tin and bake in the preheated oven for 35–40 minutes until golden.

4. Remove the cake from the oven, leave to cool in the tin for 10 minutes, then transfer to a wire rack and leave to cool completely.

5. To make the icing, spoon the solid coconut cream out of the can, leaving the milk behind. Place the cream in a bowl and beat for 2–3 minutes with a hand-held electric mixer. Sift in the icing sugar and gently mix together.

6. Cut the cake in half horizontally and spread one third of the icing over the top of one half. Place the second half on top and spread with the remaining icing. Sprinkle over the orange zest and toasted almonds and serve.

BLUEBERRY & OATMEAL MUFFINS

MAKES: *9 muffins* | **PREP:** *20 mins* | **COOK:** *20–25 mins*

INGREDIENTS

250 ml/9 fl oz pure orange juice
60 g/2¼ oz gluten-free porridge oats
100 g/3½ oz caster sugar
200 g/7 oz gluten-free plain flour,
   sifted
½ tsp xanthan gum
1½ tsp gluten-free baking powder
½ tsp gluten-free bicarbonate of
   soda
½ tsp cinnamon
¼ tsp mixed spice
125 ml/4 fl oz vegetable oil
1 egg, beaten
1 tsp glycerine
175 g/6 oz blueberries
demerara sugar, for sprinkling

1. Preheat the oven to 180°C/350°F/Gas 4. Line a 9-hole muffin tin with paper cases.

2. Add the orange juice to the oats and mix well in a bowl.

3. In a separate bowl, mix the sugar, flour, xanthan gum, baking powder, bicarbonate of soda, cinnamon and mixed spice together. Add the oil, egg and glycerine to the dry mixture and mix well to combine, then add the oat mixture and blueberries and gently fold in to the mixture.

4. Divide between the paper cases and sprinkle with demerara sugar.

5. Bake in the preheated oven for 20–25 minutes, or until a skewer inserted into the centre of a muffin comes out clean. Remove from the oven and leave to cool on a wire rack.

SEVEN-GRAIN BREAD

MAKES: *1 loaf* | **PREP:** *20 mins, plus rising* | **COOK:** *40–45 mins*

INGREDIENTS

butter, for greasing
60 g/2¼ oz amaranth flour
120 g/4¼ oz brown rice flour
120 g/4¼ oz sorghum flour
60 g/2¼ oz gluten-free cornflour
60 g/2¼ oz tapioca flour
20 g/¾ oz ground chia seeds
100 g/3½ oz milled linseeds
2 tsp xanthan gum
2 tsp gluten-free easy-blend dried
*   yeast*
1 tsp salt
3 eggs
1 tbsp vegetable oil
2 tbsp sugar
240 ml/8½ fl oz lukewarm water
10 g/¼ oz sunflower seeds

1. Grease a 450-g/1-lb loaf tin.

2. Combine the amaranth flour, brown rice flour, sorghum flour, cornflour, tapioca flour, chia seeds, linseeds, xanthan gum, yeast and salt together in a bowl.

3. In a separate bowl, mix the eggs, oil, sugar and water together until well combined. Add the dry ingredients to the egg mixture and mix well to a soft dough.

4. Put the dough into the prepared tin, sprinkle with the sunflower seeds and cover with a clean, damp tea towel. Leave to rise in a warm place for 1 hour. Preheat the oven to 180°C/350°F/Gas Mark 4.

5. Remove the tea towel and bake the loaf in the preheated oven for 40–45 minutes until golden brown. Remove from the oven and leave to cool in the tin before turning out.

SOUR CHERRY &
CINNAMON SCONES

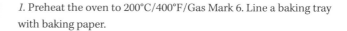

MAKES: *8 scones* | **PREP:** *15 mins* | **COOK:** *20 mins*

INGREDIENTS

250 g/9 oz gluten-free self-raising
*   flour*
1 tsp gluten-free baking powder
50 g/1¾ oz unsalted butter
50 g/1¾ oz caster sugar
50 g/1¾ oz dried cherries, chopped
½ tsp ground cinnamon
2 eggs
150 ml/5 fl oz milk
1–2 tbsp demerara sugar, for
*   sprinkling*
whipped cream and jam, to serve

1. Preheat the oven to 200°C/400°F/Gas Mark 6. Line a baking tray with baking paper.

2. Sift the flour and baking powder into a bowl. Using your fingertips, rub the butter into the flour mixture until it resembles fine breadcrumbs. Stir in the sugar, cherries and cinnamon.

3. Lightly beat one of the eggs with the milk in a separate bowl. Add to the flour mixture and beat until smooth.

4. Scoop 8 mounds of the scone mixture onto the prepared tray using a deep spoon or an ice cream scoop. Beat the remaining egg with a fork, brush a little over the top of each scone and sprinkle over the demerara sugar.

5. Bake the scones in the centre of the preheated oven for 15–18 minutes, or until they are a light golden colour. Remove the tray from the oven and slide the scones onto a wire rack to cool. Serve the scones while they are warm with cream and jam.

HORSERADISH
SODA BREAD

MAKES: *1 loaf* | **PREP:** *20 mins* | **COOK:** *45 mins*

INGREDIENTS

*500 g/1 lb 2 oz gluten-free white
    bread flour, plus extra for dusting*

*2 tsp gluten-free bicarbonate of
    soda*

1 tsp sea salt

*175 g/6 oz parsnips, peeled and
    grated*

*100 g/3½ oz mature Cheddar
    cheese, grated*

*40 g/1½ oz fresh horseradish,
    grated*

400 ml/14 fl oz buttermilk

1–2 tbsp milk (optional)

1. Preheat the oven to 200°C/400°F/Gas Mark 6.

2. Sift together the flour and bicarbonate of soda into a large mixing
bowl and stir in the salt, parsnips, cheese and horseradish. Make a
well in the centre of the mixture and pour in the buttermilk, stirring
constantly. If necessary, add 1–2 tablespoons of milk to bring the
mixture together; the dough should be soft and slightly sticky.

3. Shape the dough into a round and, using the floured handle of a
wooden spoon, create a cross on the surface by pushing the wooden
handle roughly halfway down into your uncooked loaf. Repeat to
make a cross shape.

4. Place on a baking sheet and bake in the preheated oven for 45
minutes until cooked through. Leave to cool slightly, then cut into
slices and serve.

COCONUT, CACAO & HAZELNUT TRUFFLES

MAKES: *20 pieces* | **PREP:** *25 mins* | **COOK:** *No cooking*

INGREDIENTS

85 g/3 oz unblanched hazelnuts
55 g/2 oz cacao nibs, plus an extra
  1 tbsp for coating
6 dried 'soft' figs, roughly chopped
25 g/1 oz desiccated coconut, plus
  an extra 2 tbsp for coating
1 tbsp maple syrup
finely grated rind and juice of
  ½ small orange

1. Place the hazelnuts and the cacao nibs in a food processor and process until very finely chopped.

2. Add the figs, coconut, maple syrup and orange rind and juice to the food processor and process until finely chopped and the mixture has come together in a ball.

3. Scoop the mixture out of the food processor, then cut into 20 even-sized pieces and roll each piece into a ball.

4. Finely chop the extra cacao nibs, then mix with the extra coconut on a sheet of non-stick baking paper or a plate. Roll the truffles, one at a time, in the cacao and coconut mixture, then arrange in a small plastic container. Store in the refrigerator for up to 3 days.

TAHINI CARAMEL SQUARES

MAKES: *16 squares* | **PREP:** *20 mins, plus soaking & chilling* | **COOK:** *No cooking*

INGREDIENTS

BASE

40 g/1½ oz semi-dried apples
200 g/7 oz medjool dates, stoned
100 g/3½ oz almonds
1 tsp coconut oil
¼ tsp sea salt

CARAMEL

100 g/3½ oz cashew nuts
115 g/4 oz medjool dates, stoned
4 tbsp coconut oil
2 tbsp light gluten-free tahini
3 tbsp maple syrup

CHOCOLATE TOPPING

4 tbsp coconut oil
4 tbsp maple syrup
2 tsp date syrup
4 tbsp raw cacao powder
½ tsp vanilla seeds

1. Line a 15-cm/6-inch square tin with baking paper, leaving the paper to overhang the edges by 5 cm/2 inches.

2. To make the base, soak the apple pieces in water for 5 minutes, drain and add to a food processor with the remaining ingredients. Pulse until the dates and nuts are chopped and the mixture is sticky, then spoon it into the base of the prepared tin and press down. Chill in the freezer for at least 15 minutes.

3. To make the caramel, pulse the nuts and dates in a food processor until fairly smooth. Add the oil, tahini and maple syrup and process to a smooth paste. If necessary, to make a paste of dropping consistency, add 1–2 tablespoons of water and process again. Smooth the caramel over the base and return to the freezer for 1 hour.

4. To make the chocolate topping, heat the oil, maple syrup and date syrup in a small saucepan over a medium–low heat and stir in the cacao powder and vanilla seeds. Keep stirring until you have a glossy sauce. Pour over the cold caramel and return to the freezer for 1 hour, or until the topping is firm.

5. Remove the mixture from the tin, transfer to a board and cut into 16 squares. Store in an airtight container in the refrigerator for up to 7 days.

INDEX

Melon, Parma Ham & Pecorino Salad 98

Mushrooms
Buckwheat Noodle Salad 95
Mushroom Pasta 122

Noodles
Buckwheat Noodle Salad 95
Spring Rolls 61

Nuts
Carrot & Cashew Pâté on Crackers 68
Chocolate, Cherry & Almond Fudge
Bites 173
Coconut, Cacao & Hazelnut Truffles 186
Cucumber & Buckwheat Yogurt 74
Fluffy Pancakes with Blueberries &
Almonds 24
Frisée Salad with Walnut Dressing 54
Fruit Bread with Macadamia Nuts 172
Indian Spiced Slaw 57
Jewel Salad with Ranch Dressing 52
Maple-baked Oats with Plums 18
Peachy Tofu Fool 23
Pear, Banana & Apple Breakfast Bowl 10
Pecan Pie 167
Quinoa Pizza with Cashew Cheese 105
Raw Carrot, Apple & Goji Bircher Muesli 14
Roasted Hazelnut Shortbread 175
Sweet Roots Bowl 110
Tahini Caramel Squares 188
Turkey Waldorf Bowl 88
Vanilla, Almond & Banana Smoothie 31
Very Berry Overnight Oats 17

Oats
Blueberry & Oatmeal Muffins 180
Maple-baked Oats with Plums 18
Very Berry Overnight Oats 17

Oranges
Butter Bean, Honey & Orange Cake 178
Peach & Orange Granita 164
Peachy Tofu Fool 23

Pancetta, Spinach & Chicken Salad 92

Parsnips
Creole Chicken with Coriander Parsnip
Rice 138
Horseradish Soda Bread 185
Onion & Root Vegetable Winter Roast 44
Squash & Red Pepper Pie 126

Pasta
Chicken Peperonata Bowl 135
Mushroom Pasta 122
Pancetta, Spinach & Chicken Salad 92
Pear, Banana & Apple Breakfast Bowl 10

Peas
Beef & Brassica Stir-fry 151
Pesto Salmon with Spring Veg Bowl 108

Peppers
Beef & Brassica Stir-fry 151
Buckwheat Noodle Salad 95
Chicken Peperonata Bowl 135
Creole Chicken with Coriander Parsnip
Rice 138
Poached Eggs with Tomato & Red Pepper 40
Quinoa Pizza with Cashew Cheese 105
Sausages with Red Peppers & Green
Lentils 144
Squash & Red Pepper Pie 126

Pork: Spring Rolls 61

Potatoes
Potato & Onion Frittata 37
Potato Cakes 38
Potato Salad 46
Sausage & Egg Sizzle 36
Spiced Red Cabbage & Coriander
Croquettes 58
Squash & Red Pepper Pie 126
Steak & Chips with Watercress Butter 147
Pumpkin Pie Smoothie Bowl 160

Quinoa
Black Bean & Quinoa Burritos 115
Creamy Coconut & Mango Quinoa 159
Hot Salami & Quinoa Bites with Garlic
Mayo 62
Quinoa & Beetroot Burgers 121
Quinoa Pizza with Cashew Cheese 105
Quinoa Porridge with Caramelized
Banana 12
Red Quinoa & Chickpea Salad 96

Red cabbage
Asian Salad with Coconut Rice 90
Indian Spiced Slaw 57
Red Cabbage Salad with Aubergine Dip 51
Spiced Red Cabbage & Coriander
Croquettes 58
Turkey Waldorf Bowl 88
Rhubarb & Blackberry Crumble 156

Rice
Asian Salad with Coconut Rice 90
Black Rice Pudding with Raspberry
Coulis 168
Coconut Rice Pudding with Pomegranate 161
Italian Rice with Chicken & Cherry
Tomatoes 136
Jamaican Rice & Peas with Tofu 123
Sushi Roll Bowl 111
Sweet Roots Bowl 110

Sausages
Sausage & Egg Sizzle 36
Sausages with Red Peppers & Green
Lentils 144

Seeds
Breakfast Muffins 20
Buckwheat Breakfast Bowl 8
Indian Spiced Slaw 57
Pear, Banana & Apple Breakfast Bowl 10
Pesto Salmon with Spring Veg Bowl 108
Pumpkin Pie Smoothie Bowl 160
Salmon Devilled Eggs with Black Onion
Seeds 72
Seven-grain Bread 183
Smashed Avocado with Toasted Hemp
Seeds 35
Sushi Roll Bowl 111
Sour Cherry & Cinnamon Scones 184

Spinach
Coconut Fish Curry 132
Matcha Power Smoothie 28
Mushroom Pasta 122
Pancetta, Spinach & Chicken Salad 92

Squash
Pumpkin Pie Smoothie Bowl 160
Squash & Red Pepper Pie 126
Squash, Pine Nut & Goat's Cheese Pizza 106

Sweet potatoes
Onion & Root Vegetable Winter Roast 44
Sweet Potato Rounds with Goat's Cheese
& Olives 64
Sweet Roots Bowl 110

Tofu
Jamaican Rice & Peas with Tofu 123
Peachy Tofu Fool 23

Tomatoes
Black Bean & Quinoa Burritos 115
Cauliflower & Butter Bean Stew 124
Chicken & Vegetable Soup 85
Courgette Quiche 102
Creole Chicken with Coriander Parsnip
Rice 138
Italian Rice with Chicken & Cherry
Tomatoes 136
Jewel Salad with Ranch Dressing 52
Poached Eggs with Tomato & Red Pepper 40
Quinoa Pizza with Cashew Cheese 105
Courgetti with Garlic Cream Sauce 118
Sausage & Egg Sizzle 36
Spicy Tomato, Tamarind & Ginger Soup 87
Sweet & Spicy Meatballs 148
Tomato & Bean Salsa 71
Tomato Focaccia 48

Turkey
Tamarind Turkey with Courgette
Noodles 142
Turkey Waldorf Bowl 88

Vegetable Pakoras 60

This edition published by Parragon Books Ltd in 2017
LOVE FOOD is an imprint of Parragon Books Ltd

Parragon Books Ltd
Chartist House
15–17 Trim Street
Bath BA1 1HA, UK
www.parragon.com/lovefood

ISBN 978-1-4748-6895-2

Printed in China

Edited by Fiona Biggs
Cover photography by Al Richardson

The cover shot shows the Butter Bean, Honey & Orange
Cake on page 178.

.... *Notes for the Reader* ....

This book uses both metric and imperial measurements.
Follow the same units of measurement throughout;
do not mix metric and imperial. All spoon measurements
are level: teaspoons are assumed to be 5 ml, and
tablespoons are assumed to be 15 ml. Unless otherwise
stated, milk is assumed to be full fat, eggs and individual
fruits and vegetables are medium, pepper is freshly
ground black pepper and salt is table salt. Unless
otherwise stated, all root vegetables should be peeled
prior to using.

The times given are an approximate guide only.
Preparation times differ according to the techniques used
by different people and the cooking times may also vary
from those given.

While the publisher of the book and the original author(s)
of the recipes and other text have made all reasonable
efforts to ensure that the information contained in this
book is accurate and up to date at the time of publication,
anyone reading this book should note the following
important points: -

Medical and pharmaceutical knowledge is constantly
changing and the author(s) and the publisher cannot and
do not guarantee the accuracy or appropriateness of the
contents of this book;

In any event, this book is not intended to be, and should
not be relied upon, as a substitute for appropriate, tailored
professional advice. Both the author(s) and the publisher
strongly recommend that a doctor or other healthcare
professional is consulted before embarking on major
dietary changes;

For the reasons set out above, and to the fullest extent
permitted by law, the author(s) and publisher: (i) cannot
and do not accept any legal duty of care or responsibility in
relation to the accuracy or appropriateness of the contents
of this book, even where expressed as 'advice' or using
other words to this effect; and (ii) disclaim any liability,
loss, damage or risk that may be claimed or incurred as a
consequence – directly or indirectly – of the use and/or
application of any of the contents of this book.

The publisher has been careful to select recipes that contain
gluten-free products. Any ready-made ingredients that could
potentially contain gluten have been listed as gluten free,
so readers know to check they are gluten free. However,
always read labels carefully and, if necessary, check with the
manufacturer.